PORTL
Encyclor ⁔ᴗ᠁ᴜ

Rodney Legg

Dorset Publishing Company
National School North Street Wincanton Somerset BA9 9AT

For Ben and Oliver Crabb

Publishing details
First published 1999. Copyright Rodney Legg ©1999.
Published by Dorset Publishing Company at the Wincanton Press, National School, North Street, Wincanton, Somerset BA9 9AT (01-963-32583) to whom updatings may be sent, addressed to the author. Distributed by Halsgrove, Lower Moor Way, Tiverton, Devon EX16 6SS (01-884-243-242).

Printing credits
Typeset in $10\frac{1}{2}/13$ point Caxton, by Julie Green, and illustrated with photographs from the author's collection. Printed in Somerset by F.W.B. Printing at Bennetts Mead, Southgate Road, Wincanton, Somerset BA9 9EB (01-963-33755).

International standard book number
ISBN 0 948699 56 6

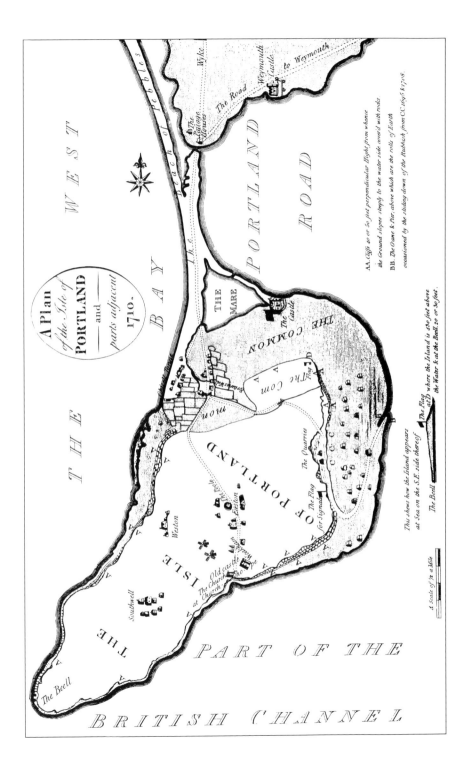

A Plan
of the Isle of
PORTLAND
and
parts adjacent
1710.

WEST

BAY

THE

ISLE

THE

PORTLAND ROAD

The Road to Weymouth

to Weymouth

Weymouth Castle

Wyke

The Passage House

Beach of Pebbles

The S.

THE MARE

THE COMMON

The Castle

THE COMMON

The Com

The Flag

OF PORTLAND

The Quarries

C.C.C.

Southwell

Weston

Old castle
The Church at Church Hope

The Flag
for Signals

The Beell

PART OF THE

BRITISH CHANNEL

AA. *Cliffs 40 or 50 feet perpendicular Hight, from whence
the Ground slopes steeply to the water side over'd with rocks*

BB. *The Crane & Pier, above which are the rolls of Earth
occasioned by the sliding down of the Rubbish from CC 1695 & 1708.*

*This shews how the Island appears
at Sea on the S.E. side thereof.*

The Flag
at D where the Island is 480 feet above
the Water & at the Beell 30 or 36 feet.

The Beell

A Scale of 1/2 a Mile

A to Z
self-indexing entries

LESLIE WARD

A

Abergavenny – an East Indiaman, outward bound, she sailed on to the Shambles sandbank off Portland Bill through a pilot's error [5 February 1805]. John Wordsworth, the commander, faced the tragic consequences with great courage and was among more than two hundred who perished. Captain Wordsworth, who was born in 1772, was the poet's brother.

William Wordsworth [1770-1850] attempted a commemorative poem but was too distressed to conclude it, though he did produce elegiac verses referring to his last parting with John, near Grisedale. There are many references to John in William's poems and the *Happy Warrior*, inspired by Nelson's death, incorporates aspects of his brother's character.

Abbotsbury Oysters – seabed pens in the shallow sheltered waters around the mouth of the Fleet lagoon at Ferrybridge.

Owned by the Ilchester Estates, headed by the Hon Charlotte Morrison, which holds the Strangways family title to the waters from here to Abbotsbury.

Admiralty Underwater Weapons Establishment – built across Barrow Hill, Southwell, Portland (SY 680 700) in 1949-52 and infamous for espionage penetration.

"The stocky 39-year-old, whose true identity may never be known, faced Lord Parker, the Lord Chief Justice, with a smile on his face, a flush on his cheeks, and the fading words of his counsel in his ears: 'At least it can be said of this man that he was not a traitor to his own

Admiralty UWE: foreground grazed by Portland sheep.

country.' But at the tone of Lord Parker's voice the smile vanished and he paled. A gasp broke the silence of the packed court at the sentence, 25 years – the longest passed there in memory."

The date was 22 March 1961, and the setting the Old Bailey, as members of the Portland spy-ring were sent down. Their "control" at the Admiralty's Underwater Weapons Establishment had been Gordon Lonsdale who was indeed no traitor to his country. The Russian's identity would, however, become known. "Lonsdale" was Colonel Conon Trimofovich Molody of the KGB. He did not stay in prison long enough to break any record, being swapped in Berlin on 21 April 1964 for Greville Wynne.

That one, we were told at the time, was an innocent British exhibition salesman, but he later turned into a self-confessed spy who had worked his Russian contact – since shot – to good account during the Cuban missile crisis.

Aircraft crashes – a Junkers Ju.88 (B3+DC) was brought down, almost undamaged, in a crash-landing at "The Castles" clifftop beside Blacknor Fort [11 August 1940]. Claimed by a Hurricane of 213 Squadron from RAF Exeter, its "B3" markings indicated it belonged to Kampfgeschwader 54, a bomber wing whose death's head emblem – Totenkopf – appeared on the fuselage just aft of the transparent nose.

The sea off Portland saw numerous casualties through the Battle of Britain and for almost the duration of the Second World War. Most of the aircraft belonged to the Luftwaffe but they were joined by many defending Spitfires and Hurricanes.

The following losses were inflicted on the Royal Air Force over the sea off Portland in Battle of Britain dog-fights:

Spitfire of 609 Squadron [9 July 1940].

Spitfires L1069 and L1095 of 609 Squadron and Hurricane N2485 of 501 Squadron [11 July 1940].

Hurricane P3084 of 501 Squadron [12 July 1940].

Spitfire K9901 of 152 Squadron [25 July 1940].

Hurricanes L2057, P3783, P3885, and R4092 of 601 Squadron [11 August 1940].

Hurricanes P3348 of 213 Squadron and P3177 of 238 Squadron [13 August 1940].

Hurricanes P2872 and P3215 of 87 Squadron [15 August 1940].

Hurricanes N2646, P2766, and P3200 of 213 Squadron, and Spitfire R6810 of 152 Squadron [25 August 1940].

Spitfire R6831 of 152 Squadron [27 August 1940].

Hurricanes P3655 and P3088 of 56 Squadron, and Spitfire L1072 of 152 Squadron [30 September 1940].

Hurricane P3421 of 56 Squadron [10 October 1940].

The following fighters were also shot down off the Dorset coast after interceptions that began over Portland:

Spitfire R6614 of 152 Squadron and Hurricane R4097 of 238 Squadron [11 August 1940].

Spitfire R6985 of 234 Squadron [15 August 1940].

German losses into the English Channel are recorded with less accuracy but the following, at least, were seen from Portland:

Junkers Ju.87 [9 July 1940].

Heinkel He.111 [15 September 1940].

Dornier Do.17 [4 January 1941].

A Royal Navy Whirlwind helicopter crashed at Portland [9 October 1968].

Another ditched in the sea at Portland Harbour [20 June 1969].

Three were killed and four saved when a Royal Navy Wessex helicopter crashed in the sea off Portland during a photographic reconnaissance exercise [20 May 1971].

The next helicopter to ditch in the sea was a Royal Navy Sea King [13 January 1972], followed a month later by a Navy Wessex, also off Portland [16 February 1972].

Alacrity – the frigate HMS *Alacrity*, on war games off Portland, was one of the first ships of the Royal Navy to be ordered to sail immediately [31 March 1982], via Plymouth, for the South Atlantic after the Argentinian invasion of the Falkland Islands.

Alex van Opstal – a 6,000-ton Belgian passenger liner, empty and homeward bound, blown up by a German mine off the Shambles Sandbank, Portland [16 September 1939]. All 49 crew and eight passengers were rescued by a Greek steamer and brought into Weymouth. The explosion was the first to be heard in south Dorset during the Second World War.

Alexander – East Indiaman, homeward bound from Bombay to London, driven high into Chesil Cove and dashed to pieces [27 March 1815]. Some 140 men, women and children were drowned; only five lascars were saved. For Portlanders, however, there was a bonanza of riches amongst the wreckage.

All Saint's Church – at Easton, behind the Straits (SY 692 718), succeeded to the rights, privileges, registers and silver of the beautiful, classical St George's, upon its completion as the replacement parish church [1916-17]. It cost £13,000.

Alleluia Bay – see entry for **Wiram Otter**.

Alma Terrace and **Alma Road** – Victorian prison officers' homes, named for the recent Battle of Alma, against the Russians in the Crimean War [20 September 1854]. Between Grove Road and the Young Offenders' Institution (SY 700 725).

Andrew – Falklands War flyer **Prince Andrew, Duke of York**, who was in the air attempting to decoy Exocet missiles when the *Atlantic Conveyor* was hit [1982], later spent a year at HMS *Osprey*, the Royal Navy's Portland helicopter flying school [1987]. For two months the Duke and Duchess rented Chideock Manor, Chideock, from publisher Charles Weld, the son of Lieutenant-Colonel Humphrey Weld and his wife Frances.

Anna Maria – Russian schooner, attempting to sail from Teignmouth to Lisbon with a cargo of china clay, but instead blown in the opposite direction by a gale [25 October 1903]. Her grave would be the Chesil Beach, at Portland, but the heavy seas also did the six-man crew a big favour. She started breaking up almost immediately and the mainmast fell sideways "forming a bridge to the shore, along which the men clambered without delaying to collect any of their belongings".

April Fools Day – see entry for the **Dreadnought Hoax**; though its date was 10 February 1910.

HMS *Argyll* – Type 23 frigate, which was the last ship of the Royal Navy to sail from Portland on the closure of the base [21 July 1995]. On board was Rear-Admiral John Tolhurst, Flag Officer Sea Training, whose 250 staff also moved to Devonport.

Armada battle – an engagement with the Spanish Armada took place off Portland Bill on Tuesday 23 July 1588. It was a lack lustre affair which achieved nothing except perhaps for the Spanish who moved on to mid-Channel and a day's sailing time nearer their Dutch interim destination without the loss of any more ships. Indeed it might have turned out a positive victory for the enemy if the day's opportunities had been taken.

Don Hugo de Moncada wanted to take advantage of the calm conditions the previous night to move his oar-powered galleasses – light but powerfully gunned highly manoeuvrable craft that were a cross between a galley and a galleon – on an attack on the English flagship. *The Ark*, eight hundred tons, had been built by Sir Walter Raleigh and sold to Queen Elizabeth I. It now carried the flag of her Lieutenant-General and Commander-in-Chief of the Navy, the Lord High Admiral of England, 52-year-old Charles Howard, Baron Howard of Effingham.

Moncada's intentions were blocked by his Commander-in-Chief, the Admiral of the ocean 38-year-old Alonso Pérez de Guzmán, seventh Duke of Medina-Sidonia. Despite a complete lack of nautical experience he was in command of the "Invincible Armada" that was undertaking this "Enterprise of England". His were the ethics of the nobleman, rooted in mediaeval chivalry, where like could fight only with like. It would only be honourable for Sidonia to engage Howard: Moncada was therefore refused permission to attack.

The initiative passed to the English. In an off-shore north-east breeze at about 5 a.m. the rash but gallant Martin Frobisher, 53-year-old veteran of the searches for the Canadian Northwest Passage, took the *Triumph* and five other ships eastward through the tricky inshore waters between the Spanish fleet and the rocks of the Portland Bill peninsula. He judged the wind perfectly and slipped into the outer waters of Weymouth Bay, between Portland Bill and St Alban's Head. No one could fault Frobisher's seamanship but his strategy was questionable – he had chosen to box himself into a corner.

Howard hesitated about following. He was too cautious to risk placing *The Ark* between the enemy and the rocks and held back his cluster of vessels. The Armada's rearguard, led by de Leyva, Oquendo and Bertendona, closed in to attempt boardings as Sidonia himself swung towards the action. Howard also seemed to be closing for a fight as he led his line of England's biggest ships towards the *San Martin*. They came to within a hundred or 120 yards according to the accounts of both sides. Purser Pedro Calderon's published *Relacion* of the action is that the *San Martin* withstood considerable fire: "The enemy shot at the Duke at least 500 cannon-balls, some of which struck the hull and others his rigging, carrying away his flagstaff and one of the stays of the mainmast." Fifty were killed.

The damage, however, was not critical. Neither was that which the *San Martin* inflicted upon Howard's ships, even though Calderon says she "fired over eighty shots from one side only, and inflicted great damage". He realised, however, that the engagement was essentially a failure as the Spanish were constantly "trying to come up with them" and failing to close-in sufficiently on the English vessels. There was also a missing element of luck: the Spaniard's heavier 50-pound cannon-balls failed to smash *The Ark's* rigging.

Meanwhile Frobisher's division of the English fleet was potentially isolated. Sir Francis Drake saw its quandary and was in no mood to take the *Revenge* inshore to join them. Frobisher, however, could not be under-estimated. He set about showing that the galleasses could not take on standard sized warships in a straight fight and used his great galleon – the *Triumph* was just about the largest ship from either England or Spain – to smash his way out of trouble. Instead of closing sufficiently to try and hole their hulls he used his massive fire-power to rake the rowing decks of the galleasses and immobilise both the oarsmen and their oars. Moncada had to revert to sails and thereby lost the whole manoeuvring advantage of the galleasses. None of the cornered English vessels would be lost and the Spaniards had taken a mauling in an attack which they were now forced to abandon.

By noon the wind had strengthened and backed to the south-west. It carried with it, fast up-Channel, 50 English vessels spearheaded by Drake in the Revenge. Howard realised that the initiative was now his and once again attacked the San Martin. Drake went for the rearguard commander, Juan Martinez de Recalde, his principal target of previous engagements, but once again Recalde could count on his other vessels for support. The Armada was able to return to its formations and use the south-west wind to take it on past St Alban's Head and towards the Isle of Wight.

It is easier to disentangle the individual actions that make up the Armada story than to explain the venture as a whole. This first great clash of western empires came about because of a schism in Christendom: Spanish southern Europe was taking on Protestant northern Europe. In world terms it was the Spanish not the English who were the megapower for Philip II ruled over the first empire upon which the sun never set. It covered much of the Americas, and since 1580 had incorporated Portugal's possessions there and in West Africa, Ceylon and the East Indies. Its nearer reaches included Sardinia, Milan, and Naples and Sicily. The key to the Armada escapade was that beyond the English Channel lay the Spanish Netherlands; a tenuous union of Holland, Belgium and Luxembourg.

There was no natural animosity between the English and the Spanish, bar competitive strains of trade with the New World. England's hereditary enemy was France. War with the French had been, and would be again, the national game for half the millennium.

The Spanish tussle was a direct result of religious interference in politics and began when an Englishman, Cardinal Allen, persuaded the Pope to

Excommunicate Elizabeth I in 1570 and declare her to be "deprived of her pretended title of the kingdom". The English became an annoyance to Spain with the piracy of Drake, Hawkins and Elizabeth's other sea-dogs, and the chance impounding of Italian cash, destined for the Netherlands, in a ship which had been forced into an English port by rough seas. Then by flinging out the Sea-beggars – exiled Netherlands nationalists who had sought refuge in England – Elizabeth was the catalyst for their war of independence against Spain.

Brill and Flushing were captured by the Sea-beggars and England came to be regarded as the cause and succour of the revolution in the Netherlands. Don John of Austria called on Philip II for action: "Everyone believes that the only remedy to the disorders of the Netherlands is for England to be ruled by someone devoted to your Majesty. If the contrary case prevails it will lead to the ruin of those countries and their loss to your Crown."

It happened that there was in Mary Queen of Scots a claimant to the English throne. At home Elizabeth feared plots and across the water the situation in the Netherlands had improved significantly for the Spanish. French help to the rebels ceased in 1584 with the death of the Duke of Alençon ("My Frog" Elizabeth used lovingly to call him)

and the assassination of William the Silent who had been leading the Sea-beggars.

Elizabeth was not prepared to see Spain wipe Protestant resistance from the Netherlands. She sent in English troops. Mary Queen of Scots meantime did something naive, inept and incredibly stupid. In a letter smuggled out of prison she committed herself not only as a contender for Elizabeth's throne but promised to re-establish Catholicism. It would be intercepted and read by Elizabeth's spy-master, Secretary of State Sir Francis Walsingham. There was but one punishment for the highest treason.

The news that Mary had been beheaded convinced Philip, who had long deliberated an "Enterprise of England", the mount the invasion. The order was sent from his vast Escorial palace to the Captain-General for Ocean Seas to build a huge troop-carrying fleet. This Armada was dealt its first crippling blow before it had even assembled at Lisbon for the voyage.

Sir Francis Drake began the "singeing of the King of Spain's beard" – Drake's own words for it – at four o'clock in the afternoon of Wednesday 24 April 1857 and continued his orgy of destruction at Cadiz for twenty hours. He left between 24 (the enemy's admission) and 37 vessels (the English claim) as burnt-out hulks. They included Santa Cruz's flagship.

Drake proceeded to carry out a brilliant pre-emotive strike against the Spanish logistical preparations. At Cape St Vincent he captured bulk supplies of barrel hoops and staves that were en route for Lisbon; this denied the enemy vital packaging capacity for the food and drink required for the expedition.

Then to cap it all Drake intercepted and brought home the Portuguese *San Felipe*, worth £114,000 which was and would remain the most valuable ship ever captured on the high seas.

For all that, Drake knew he had only delayed the moment when the Armada would sail; but he had given time for English preparations.

As a plan the Armada contained the seeds of failure by demanding double jeopardy. Firstly the fleet of 130 ships, with 10,000 sailors and 19,000 soldiers, were not heading for England but making a Channel dash past England to the Netherlands. There they were tasked to link up with the Duke of Parma's army, with its 30,000 infantry and 4,000 cavalry being decanted into barges, and escort them to England. Such an extended operation relied upon the weather co-operating for far longer than could be predicted and indeed required against the odds for the winds to permit two totally different fleet movements.

Having taken the weather for granted the Spanish showed a similar blindness towards the English. It was monumental self-deception for the enemy to believe that religion would outweigh prudence and patriotism; that when the Armada came into sight England would be thrown into civil war with a spontaneous uprising of the Catholic 35 percent of the population. In the event there was no evidence that a single Catholic family took up arms against their Queen.

History is full of arguable "ifs" – but the success of the Spanish Armada is not one of them. Even with hindsight it remains an untenable scenario.

Arrowroot – see entry for **Portland Sago**.

Arum neglectum – known as Portland Sago, this lush version of Cuckoo-pint was grown and marketed on the island in the 18th century. It was used as a common starch and cosmetic.

L' Atlantique – France's flagship luxury liner became a blazing inferno three miles east-south-east of Portland Bill [5 January 1933]. Evacuated and empty she seemed set to become Dorset's most spectacular shipwreck of all time.

The Daily Mail's Weymouth correspondent arrived at sunrise on Portland Bill: "As the news spread excited watchers on shore came and saw billows of smoke pouring from the vessel high into the skies, and shimmering waves of heat arose around her from the glowing hull. British, French and Dutch tugs circled about her, their crews trying to get a line aboard and bring her under control.

"For six hours the heat and smoke held them at bay, and the *Atlantique*, uncontrolled and helpless, was until late in the afternoon a plaything of the tide, the north-west wind, and dangerous Channel currents."

The current was bringing her closer: "Fears ran high near midday that the *Atlantique* would drift inside the Shambles bank, and on the turning of the tide be borne aground somewhere on the Dorset shore."

It did not happen: "Almost imperceptibly, however, she drifted away from Portland and out into the Channel.

"She presented a pitiful spectacle at close quarters. She listed heavily to port and her bows dipped; her hull was red hot above the water line; parts of her interior were bared to the air and her foremast lay across her ruined deck. All that remained of her palatial 'street' of shops and other lavish equipment were unrecognisable remnants.

"It was late in the afternoon that the men from the tugs, braving the heat and choking smoke, got aboard her. A Frenchman was the first to do so, and the first thing he did was to hoist a French ensign on the ruined monster's remaining mast."

Several hours more passed before hawsers were successfully secured, and once the boarding party retreated with their lives as the fire erupted again. There was the financial motive for the determination: "Though the burning liner came so near Weymouth, it was decided to take the risk of towing her back across the Channel rather than beach her on the English shore, where heavy salvage charges would have been incurred."

Because of her heavy list she had to be towed broadside: "At 4.45 I saw her slowly disappear on the horizon near St Alban's Head – the rearguard of a slow, sad procession. Forty hours after she had caught fire she was still burning furiously deep down in her tortured hull."

From off Purbeck, the *Atlantique* was slowly towed through the night, southwards, on the 80 mile journey to Cherbourg. She was to make it home, against all the adversity.

The fire had started when the liner was off the Casquets, in the Channel Islands, and from there she had drifted to the eastern edge of Lyme Bay – and what would have been thence to the rocks of Portland or Purbeck if lines had not been attached before nightfall.

Throughout her long drift across the Channel and then back again, she was shadowed by the French minelayer *Pollux*, with guns and torpedo tubes ready to sink the liner if she became a danger to other shipping.

Avalanche – 1,160-ton three masted Shaw Saville Line clipper which sank off Portland Bill after colliding with the *Forest* [11-12 September 1877], with the loss of 106 lives. Many were New Zealand émigrés, outward bound from London, including colonists who were going back again after a holiday visiting friends and relations in "the old country".

She is commemorated by St Andrew's Avalanche Memorial Church, at Southwell, with her huge

Avalanche clipper: her anchor, beside the Memorial Church at Southwell.

recovered anchor set beside it. See the entry for this church.

Avice's Cottage – at the south end of Wakeham, Portland, on the east side of the wide street (SY 696 713). It was given to the island by birth control pioneer Dr Marie Stopes and, with the contemporary cottage adjoining, became Portland Museum [1930].

Avice's Cottage has a 1640 datestone – when it was built by Bartholomew Mitchell – an 18th century stone fireplace, and a thatched roof. The other cottage is much the same and the two are now one building.

It has the distinction, because of its thatch which is such a rarity on Portland, of being incorporated by Thomas Hardy into his novel *The Well-Beloved* [magazine serial 1892; book version 1897], as the home of would-be well-beloved Avice Caro, who dies and is followed by two other unattainable Avices.

"All men are pursuing a shadow," Hardy said later, in defence of his improbable plot.

B

Balaclava Bay – created in Victorian times by the building of the Inner Breakwater of Portland Harbour and lying seaward of it at

Avice's Cottage: a Hardy setting for Portland Museum.

the north-east corner of the island (SY 699 742). Named for the Battle of Balaclava which saw the famous Charge of the Light Brigade in the Crimean War [25 October 1854].

Balfour – fraudster **Jabez Balfour**, the Burnley MP whose group of companies collapsed in 1892, was Britain's greatest economic criminal of the 19th century.

He was extradited from Argentina to stand trial at the Old Bailey and served the first 18 months of his 14-year sentence with hard labour on Portland.

Convict V.460 arrived at the awesome buildings of The Grove aware of his predicament: "There was no necessity to carve the words 'Abandon hope, all ye who enter

here' over the entrance to Portland Prison. The massive, cold grey walls say that for themselves."

Battle of Portland – hardly a "famous victory", as has been claimed, but nearly a disaster for both the English and Dutch fleets as they fought off Portland Bill [18 February 1653]. Admiral Robert Blake [1599-1657] was lucky to escape with his life, and Maarten Harpertszoon Tromp [1597-1653] was fortunate to survive with the bulk of his ships.

Blake blundered by taking his red squadron alone to intercept Tromp's full fleet. The English flagship, the *Triumph*, was heavily engaged, with the loss of its captain, and Blake was severely wounded.

Not until the afternoon did Vice-Admiral Sir William Penn [1621-70] arrive with the blue and white squadrons of the English fleet to make an even battle. By next morning the ships were off St Catherine's Point, Isle of Wight, and Tromp escaped up Channel. He had lost five warships sunk and four captured, and 40 merchant ships were also lost, but the main Dutch fleet survived to fight again.

Beacon Quarry – the disused stone workings at Portland Bill, which have left Pulpit Rock standing proud (SY 676 683) as the island's south-western seamark [circa 1875]. Named for an Armada-period beacon site.

The Beale – the old name for Portland Bill, it being described as "Beale Point (vulgarly called the Bill)" in John Hutchins' county history [1774].

Bedford – chief test pilot **Alfred William (Bill) Bedford** [born 1920] achieved the first vertical landing by a fixed wing aircraft on an aircraft-carrier when he brought his Hawker Siddeley P 1127 Kestrel, prototype of the Harrier, down on HMS *Ark Royal* as she sailed at 5-knots to the east of The Shambles, Portland Bill [8 February 1963].

Bill Lighthouse – see entry for **Portland Bill**.

Bird Observatory – see entry for **Portland Bird Observatory**.

HMS ***Bittern*** – destroyer which "went down like a stone," taking all her crew with her, on being rammed by the steamship *Kenilworth* [03.15 hours, 4 April 1918]. The collision occurred south-west of Portland Bill. Fog was gleamed and no lights were being shown due to the danger of enemy submarines, with the steamer being blamed for sailing too far out in the English Channel on its course towards Start Point.

Blacknor Fort – four 9.2-inch guns were installed during the First World War in this Victorian emplacement midway along Portland's western clifftop (SY 679 717) in a commanding position overlooking Lyme Bay. Anti-aircraft rockets, using 3-inch tubular charges produced by the Royal Naval Cordite Factory, Holton Heath, were tested here [1937-39], by the Explosives Research Department of the Royal Arsenal, Woolwich.

Gun-laying predictors monitored the fall of shot in an extended series of successful proving trials. These were discontinued and moved to Aberporth, Wales, when it became clear that Blacknor would be needed by the Army for the duration of the emergency that was developing into the Second World

War. The rockets went into production with a 25-lb shell, both for anti-aircraft salvoes of 19 rockets in a cluster, and for air to ground anti-ship purposes. An improvised version had a 60-lb warhead for use against tanks, railway locomotives and other land targets. The rockets were also used for assisting aircraft to take off from merchant ships.

Blacknor Fort saw one of Portland's most remarkable pieces of aerial combat in the Battle of Britain. Beside it, on "The Castles" as Portlanders call the flat top of the 275-feet cliffs, Flying Officer Strickland, in a Hurricane of 213 Squadron from Exeter, bagged a German bomber in style on the afternoon of 11 August 1940.

His Hurricane fighter crippled the Junkers Ju.88 which then made an almost perfect landing, but for the fact it snagged the fort's line of telephone wires, which retracted the undercarriage. The pilot was injured but his three comrades had only superficial knocks and the aircraft flopped down just about intact.

The gunners of Blacknor witnessed the so-called Slapton Sands Massacre, of more than 600 American soldiers and seamen, on the night of 27 April 1944. They were ordered not to engage the German E-boats that had perpetrated the sinkings of the tank landing ships, because of the number of men who were swimming and drowning in Lyme Bay.

HMS **Blackwood** – frigate of the Royal Navy's 3rd Escort Group, sunk off Portland by a torpedo from German submarine *U-764* [19.11 hours, 15 June 1944]. The bows and stern of the ship were left jutting upwards from the water and the wreck remained afloat almost until dawn, when radar contact was lost [04.10 hours, 16 June 1944]. There were heavy casualties and 35 of the survivors were wounded.

HMS **Boadicea** – a Royal Navy destroyer, sunk off Portland with the loss of almost all aboard, by a Junkers Ju.188 bomber that released two aerial torpedoes into her port side [04.45 hours, 13 June 1944]. The second hit her forward magazine and the resultant explosion removed the front half of the ship, leaving the stern to inundate and sink within minutes. Only 12 of her crew survived, being picked up by HMS *Vanquisher* and taken to Portland.

The destroyer had been escorting convoy EBC8, and was zig-zagging at 9 knots at the time the bomber attacked. It was initially mistaken for a friendly RAF Beaufighter.

Boat-hauls – derricks used to winch fishing boats in and out of the sea, from the top of the sheer cliffs

Boat-hauls: derricks on Portland's south-east cliffs.

on the south-east side of the island. Red Crane is closest to Portland Bill (SY 680 685) and others are beside Limekiln Cave (SY 689 696) and at God Nore (SY 691 698). They were former quarry winches.

HMS *Boscawen* – third-rate 70-gun wooden battleship, with triple masts and rigging, which served in the Baltic Fleet during the Crimean War [1854-55] and was pensioned off to the newly-constructed Portland Harbour as a Royal Navy cadet Training Ship [1866]. Stood-down and re-named HMS *Wellesley* [1873].

Replaced by the first-rate, 4,579-ton battleship HMS *Trafalgar*, also 70-guns but more recently built [1841], and a veteran of action off the Crimea peninsula with the Black Sea Fleet [1855]. Re-named HMS *Boscawen* [1873].

Joined by two first-generation new style ironclad battleships, each of 10,600-tons, with the first being HMS *Minotaur* [1893], which earlier in her career entered Portland Harbour as flagship of the Channel Fleet [1877]. She was re-named HMS *Boscawen II*, and joined by HMS *Agincourt*, re-named HMS *Boscawen III* [1902].

By now there was also a land-based Boys' Training Establishment on the north-eastern slopes of the island [established 1892]. The whole operation carried the name HMS *Boscawen* and housed a total of 1,600 "Navy boys".

The ships were removed [1905-07] and replaced by the cruiser HMS *Sapphire* and a succession of smaller training brigs – with one gun deck, two high masts, and a funnel at the centre – such as HMS *Martin* and HMS *Seaflower*, which had been regular visitors to the harbour since the turn of the 20th century.

Bound Stone – marks the claims of Portlanders to four miles of the Chesil Beach, north-westwards from Chiswell, Portland, at a point opposite Lynch Cove where The Fleet Lagoon widens at Chickerell (SY 635 785). It must be one of the least visited spots on earth. A new stone was lowered into position by a Royal Navy Wessex helicopter in 1974.

Traditionally, a Court Leet and island dignitaries "Go out Bound Stone" on Ascension Day, once every seven years. There "according to ancient custom, time out of mind" they "well and truly establish the bounds of the Royal Manor of Portland". On the other side of the stone the parish of Chickerell has claim to the next three-quarters of a mile of pebbles.

Bournemouth – the paddle-steamer that carried the new resort's name was wrecked on the western side of Portland Bill, beneath the Higher Lighthouse [27 August 1886].

Her bows stuck firm on the inshore rocks and all aboard were lowered to safety. Efforts failed to prise her clear and she was then battered to pieces by a series of westerly gales.

Bow and Arrow Castle – see entry for **Rufus Castle**.

Boys' Training Establishment – the successor to HMS *Boscawen*, established in Portland Harbour aboard the retired battleships HMS *Colossus* and HMS *Collingwood* [22 September 1921]. Both vessels were withdrawn the following year.

Bound Stone: lowered into place.

Methodist chapel at Fortuneswell [1792-93].

Brackenbury Memorial Church – towards the top of the main street in Fortuneswell (SY 689 734), built [1903] in memory of Robert Carr Brackenbury [1752-1818] of Wakeham, Portland, and Raithby Hall, Lincolnshire. It replaced an earlier chapel that had been built by Brackenbury [1792-93].

Brackenbury – pastor **Robert Carr Brackenbury** [1752-1818] visited Dorset in 1791 and was told: "The island of Portland is all darkness; you must go there." He took on the burden of countering their disbelief and "at his sole expense" built a

Bristow – helicopter pilot **Lieutenant Alan Bristow** [born 1923], of 771 Naval Air Squadron, brought down his Fleet Air Arm Sikorski R4B Hoverfly on to the makeshift floorboarded flight-deck of trials ship *K253*, the frigate HMS *Helmsdale*, off Portland [6 September 1946]. It was the first helicopter landing on a naval escort-vessel at sea. Bristow would

'Bournemouth' steamer: failed to round Portland Bill in 1886.

become chairman of the Bristow Helicopter Group [1967].

Brodick Castle – replacement paddler-steamer for the *Bournemouth*, which had been wrecked at Portland Bill, [1886]. She in turn would sink within sight of her predecessor's grave [1910] whilst embarking on her maiden transatlantic voyage as an Argentinian cattle barge

Brown – hero **Cyril Brown** of the Fortuneswell Lifesaving Company was awarded the Stanhope Medal for the bravest deed of 1944. See entry for ***LCT A2454***.

Burt – Weymouth **Detective-Constable Leonard Burt** set in motion the process that would trap the Portland spies, after a tip-off that naval base worker Harry Houghton was making regular visits to the Polish embassy in London [autumn 1959]. Burt would become the county's Assistant Chief Constable and retired to Ferndown.

The Butts – the island's mediaeval archery ranges from the Battery above Red Pools (SY 683 688) inland for 400 yards, to the road at Harpland, north-east of the former Lower Lighthouse.

Bynnenḍyk – Dutch freighter, returning to Rotterdam from New York, blown up by a German mine

off the Shambles Sandbank, Portland [7 October 1939]. The 42 crew abandoned the blazing wreck and watched her sink from their rescue vessel, which took them to Weymouth.

C

Caro – three generations of this fictional Portland family – name **Avice Caro**, daughter **Ann Avice Caro**, and grand-daughter **Avice Caro** – are Thomas Hardy's vision of the perfect woman in his novel *The Well-Beloved* [1892].

Castles – see entries for **Portland Castle** and **Rufus Castle**, also the mock-fortification **Pennsylvania Castle**.

The Castles – flat-topped headland beside Blacknor Fort (SY 679 717).

Castletown – Victory Road leads up to Cadets Corner, where Castle Road is overlooked by Boscawen House, with military ownership proclaimed by an Admiralty "33" boundary marker, up from the old cemetery (SY 684 740).

Next is Portland Hospital, where Castletown begins, spread inland from Royal Naval Air Station Portland. To the left, giving the naval town its name, is Henry VIII's best preserved seaside fort, Portland Castle.

A roundabout now lies at what in Victorian times was the intersection with the Merchants' Railway, leading to the former stone quays. The naval implants are Admiralty Landing and the Coaling Pier and Coaling Camber at the entrance to the Royal Navy Dockyard.

Its strand is called The Strip, with the Jolly Sailor and the 1898-dated tiled frontage of the Portland Roads Hotel. There follows the Royal Breakwater Hotel and The Albert, now called the Green Shutters, and the Sailors' Return; awaiting a different comeback as it is boarded-up at the time of writing. The offices of HMS *Osprey* stand to the south-east of the roundabout.

Beyond Castletown is the Dockyard, with some surviving buildings of The Depot at Admiralty Slaughter House of Victorian times, and former Balaclava Coastguard Station beside Balaclava Bay, just outside the Inner Breakwater and named for the famous battle of the Crimean War.

Cave Hole – sea cave beneath the coast path half a mile north-east of Portland Bill (SY 687 690). Blow holes stretch far into the solid rock. You can look down into it from above, through the fissures, but without sensing its true proportions. The interior cavern is 50 feet square and 21 feet high.

Small craft have been driven into

Castletown hostelries: a Victorian view of The Strip with lerrets beached beside it.

it by south-easterly gales. The largest was a 40-ton vessel from Cowes in 1780. Formerly the name of the cave was "Keeve's" and it figures in many of Portland's smuggling tales, with the legends being kept alive by an eerie boom from beneath the ground during heavy seas.

It is particularly dangerous and dramatic in an easterly gale when the sea snorts up through fissures beside the path in a series of blow-holes.

Cement – see entry for **Portland cement**.

The Cenotaph – the empty tomb in London's Whitehall, this comprises great blocks from the Portland whitbed; cut, rubbed and gritted to shape. It is 35 feet high and weighs 120 tons, with joints that are the finest to have been worked on stone since the Parthenon was built above Athens in the 5th century BC. The other subtlety of design is that it does not contain a single vertical or horizontal line.

Every piece of stone was cut slightly out of true and if the apparent verticals are extended they meet at a point 1,000 feet into the sky. The horizontal-looking surfaces and joins are circumferentials of an imaginary circle that has its centre 900 feet beneath the ground.

This design was the creation of Sir Edwin Lutyens [1869-1944], though not originally as a column of stone but as a sketch for a temporary wooden saluting base that took him only a matter of hours to devise. The platform was needed for a march of troops through London in the peace celebrations of July 1919.

On 30 July 1919 Bonar Law's War Cabinet ordered the replacement of the temporary structure with a permanent replica. The massive white blocks were cut from the northern side of the Perryfield Quarries, on the western part of the land in the angle of old railway cuttings opposite the Mermaid Inn and Portland Museum at the

The Cenotaph: Portland stone.

Chesil Beach: the Cove House Inn, its closest building.

Chesil Beach: the famous view from Verne Yeates.

Pennsylvania Castle end of Wakeham's wide street (SY 695 712) under two little fields known as Pitt's Ground and Above Coombe.

The construction was carried out by Holland, Hannen and Cubitts Ltd at a cost of £7,325. Lutyens waived any fee for his most famous work. It was unveiled by King George V on Armistice Day, 11 November, in 1920.

Cherbourg bombardment – carried out by Rear Admiral Deyo's Portland Task Force [25 June 1944]. Split into two formidable bombardment groups, the fleet comprised three battleships – United States Ships *Texas*, *Arkansas*, and *Nevada* – and four cruisers, protected by nine destroyer escorts.

Chesil Beach – a great ridge of a hundred million tonnes of shingle that extends from West Bay (formerly from Golden Cap) to Portland, growing in height and content-size all the way eastwards. It would appear to be globally unique, in that despite exploration and satellite photograph no one has found a beach quite like it.

This wonder of the geological world is the classic tombolo – a spit joined to land at both ends. Denys Brunsden and Andrew Gourie observe in their Geographical Association guide to Dorset: "It is remarkable for its size, its regular crest line, its beautifully even curve, its lack of lateral ridges, its oft-quoted grading of pebble sizes. As a result, it is the most written about of all landforms in Britain."

The gravel at the West Bay end is the sort you find in fish-tanks. By the time the beach reaches Portland it is composed of oval pebbles the size of saucers (called 'cobbles'). This phenomenon of the graduation of material into size by the action of water is called alutriation and can be replicated in a laboratory. 'Chesil' was the old English word for pebble.

In these 18 miles the beach rises in stature as it goes, from a flat start, to 23 feet at Abbotsbury, and 40 feet at Portland. It came into existence about 80,000 years ago, at a time of low sea levels – caused by the Ice Age (the Devensian glacial) which 'locked' water into glaciers – and was then a couple of miles into the Channel. It seems that the island of Portland must be the clue to its survival, acting as a huge groyne.

The materials were from a raised beach at Portland, and the gravels of an extinct river that ran along The Fleet, rendered available to wave-action after the sea had broken through and captured the valley. The action of the sea proceeded to grade the materials into a sequence of general eastwards growth, with the result that local fishermen landing in fog know their location to the nearest mile. The beach mainly comprises flint and chert, with quartzites, a little local limestone, and odd stones from deposits as far west as Cornwall. These last stones could only have been acquired when the beach was further out to sea.

Towards Portland the crest-line of the beach can sometimes be moulded by a storm into ridges and gullies but these are temporary features.

Seepage, washing out pebbles from the base, and the rolling of shingle from the crest, is causing the beach to continue its slow advance towards the mainland, lessening the width of the Fleet, at a rate of a yard or so per century.

The shorter term man-made threat is shingle extraction. Scientific evidence shows that the Chesil Beach is a finite resource; it is not being replenished by some shingle-making process out of the sea. Exploitation of the Chesil Beach at the 1970s rate of 27,000 tonnes a year would see it all removed in 3,000 years, and start to cause coastal flooding nearer our time.

This is not an environment for human survival. In the age of sail countless ships were driven by the south-westerlies, unbroken from the Atlantic, into the angle of the bank and Portland, which became known as Deadman's Bay. Before the use of rocket-fired lines there was no escape from the swirling pebbles. Even on a normal day there is an undertow that exhausts swimmers. Above the water, climbing up and down can be painfully difficult.

Some masochists like Roland Gant have walked eight miles along the beach from Abbotsbury, to prove Portland is not quite an island. If you want to do likewise allow a full eight-hour walking day. It is going to be too wild for comfort if south-westerly winds of force eight and upwards are forecast for Portland, and bitterly slow against a cold easterly in winter. A force eleven hurricane from the south-west coinciding with a particularly high tide causes waves to break over the top of the bank. So listen to the shipping forecast on Radio 4 before you set off.

And also respect the rights of the little tern! It is listed in schedule one of the Wildlife and Countryside Act 1981 which makes it an offence "if any person intentionally disturbs" it "while it is building a nest or is in or near a nest containing eggs or young". Strangways Estates agent E. W. S. Green says: "I would like to take the opportunity of pointing out that the Chesil Beach is closed during the nesting season – 1 May to 31 August. Both Strangways Estates and the Crown Commissioners, the owners of the Bank, welcome visitors outside the nesting season but would be grateful for your assistance in publicising the controls exercised in this important sea-bird nesting area."

Gold coins are still occasionally washed up on the Chesil Beach but no longer in the quantity recorded by the Dorset County Chronicle of 18 December 1828: "Many of the Portland Islanders, as well as others, will be enabled to enjoy the Christmas holidays most merrily, from the effects of the late high tide and heavy gales of wind, which have been the means of throwing up on the beach bars of gold and silver. Guineas, crowns and dollars are picked up in abundance, which have been buried in the sea for many years from the various shipwrecks; the old adage 'It is a bad wind that blows no-one good' is thus amply verified."

What colour is the Chesil Beach if all the pebbles are washed away? Blue is the answer, or bluish-grey to be precise. Not that anyone in the 20th century has been able to vouch for this, from personal experience, but in Victorian times it was a known fact.

One of the most remarkable Chesil Beach phenomena took place in 1841 when a groundswell "laid bare for miles" the blue Kimmeridge Clay beneath the pebbles. Beachcombing, recovering the losses of ancient wrecks, thrived and people found antique rings, seals, silver, gold ingots and coins. Roman coins were "most numerous" – especially the third-bronze of Constantine. A strong north-easterly wind had swept the shingle from the clay and the stones were not pushed back until the next south-westerlies.

In November 1853 it was estimated that more than four million tons of shingle were swept into the sea during storms.

Chesil Beach Bound Stone – beating the bounds ceremonies were revived in the 20th century as colourful anachronisms for children and the cameras but Portlanders, with their traditional disdain for mainlanders, or 'kimberlins' as they called us, never neglected their boundary. Being almost an island they have but one, on a bleak wind-swept section of Chesil Beach pebbles at the point where the East Fleet lagoon begins to widen two miles north-west from its Small Mouth entrance. From Small Mouth to here (SY 644 776) the Chesil Beach is part of the parish of Portland. It then enters the parish of Chickerell.

Bounds used to be beaten so that children would learn at an impressionable age, via a stroke of the cane across the buttocks, the point beyond which they were not allowed to stray. In mainland Dorset such boundaries were generally marked by thick hedgerows that – until the post-war farming revolution of this century – had been serving the purpose since Saxon times. In the Portland case, as in featureless landscapes of other types, stones were necessary to demarcate the line.

Such things used to be taken very seriously. The commination against sinners in the 16th century Prayer Book includes: "Cursed is he that removeth away the mark of his neighbour's land."

Portlanders have over the ages used their energy and expertise to replace the marker stones in this inhospitable nothingness – for the practical purpose of reasserting their claim to the fishing rights and the free use of the beach of hauling ashore the shoals of mackerel. They had the job easy in 1974 when a Royal Navy helicopter of 516 Squadron dropped the new stones into position.

The Bridport News of May 1893 recorded a better attended ceremony and challenged a few of the Portlanders' assumptions:

"The Portlanders seem determined to keep up their rights, which they annually maintain by an official visit to the well-known 'bound-stone' on the Chesil Beach. Holy Thursday, or Ascension Day, is, as by custom, the day on which the ceremony takes place. This year the number attending seems to have been augmented for some reason or other; perhaps the fact of

a new stone being used added importance to the affair. Be that as it may, there were many visitors, both by sea and land.

"It is said the rights of Portlanders extend to the new bound stone opposite Fleet, but the public would like to be enlightened as to the nature of those rights. There is one right at all events which does not extend beyond the Portland side of the stone, that is, we are informed that the lord of the manor of Abbotsbury, or rather the Earl of Ilchester, does not interfere with or claim the foreshore. Not that such a right would be of any use whatever, seeing the difficulty of telling where it is. The shingle shifts with the weather, and with it the foreshore, if ever such existed except in fertile imagination."

Cheyne Weare – 1.5 acre clifftop picnic area on a dramatic slant with panoramic views from Portland's eastern quarrylands of Southwell Road (SY 693 704). It is part of the Southwell landslip of 1665.

The former spoil tip was cleaned up by ARC Southern and provided with stone benches facing seawards, looking over Weymouth Bay to St Alban's Head and the Isle of Wight.

Then the construction company presented the land to Portland town council in 1987 on a peppercorn rent of £1 a year. "Cheyne Weare has been the best place for

generations for the island's fishermen to spot shoals of mackerel," quarry manager John Reay said at the handover ceremony.

Old Chiswell: cottages and fisher-folk, seen in 1938.

Chiswell – the waterside hub of old Portland, below Fortuneswell, clustered around Chesil Cove (SY 684 724). Promenade sea defences defend the waterfront Cove House Inn, with Clark's Boat Works, the Little Ship, and Royal Victoria Hotel in the densely built hinterland.

Chiswell Sea-wall – sea defence of concrete-faced stone built [1958-65] to protect the community at the southern end of the Chesil Beach, Portland, where some 30 acres of the West Cliff had slipped into the West Weares undercliff [1859].

Christian's Fleet – wrecked in Deadman's Bay, as West Bay and

Chesil Cove became known, in the biggest group loss of shipping to take place in Dorset waters [16 November 1795].

Rear-Admiral Sir Hugh Cloberry Christian [1747-98] set sail from Spithead, into a wind that became a hurricane. They were tasked to sail to the West Indies, where Sir Hugh was to take over as Commander-in-Chief, but few of the vessels reached a point between Portland and Bridport, and none any further. The flagship, the 98-gun *Prince George*, limped back to Portsmouth with her rigging smashed and unseaworthy almost beyond repair.

The less fortunate craft foundered or were driven ashore and 1,000 men were estimated to have drowned. Two hundred bodies were washed up along the Chesil Beach.

Christiana – Norwegian barque, carrying floorboards from Drammen to Dartmouth, thrown spectacularly into Chesil Cove by a hurricane, drowning two of her crew of ten [2 September 1883].

Church Ope Cove – the picturesque but stony east-facing little bay tucked away beneath Rufus Castle and the ruined mediaeval church of St Andrew, reached by a dramatic flight of steps (SY 697 710). Rows of beachhuts are crammed into everywhere suitable for a flat space between the top of the beach and the sheer cliffs.

Named firstly for the old church and secondly for the "Ope" which was local dialect for "an opening in the cliffs down to the water's edge", according to Dorset's Victorian parson-poet philologist William Barnes. "Cove" sums up its other attribute; the small, rounded bay. "Churchhope" was its name as long ago as 1710.

The beach and rugged cliffs are registered common land [part of CL2] which is reached by public footpaths number 18 (from the Museum and Rufus Castle), 96 (from Pennsylvania Castle via the ruined church), 65 (from Cheyne Weare), with path 19, beside the beachhuts, linking these.

Clarke – Irish rebel **Thomas J. Clarke** convicted under the name of Wilson, arrived at Portland Prison – the buildings at The Grove which are now the Young Offenders' Institution – in 1884 with a life sentence for conspiring with the Fenian or Irish Revolutionary Brotherhood to Dynamite public buildings in England. He was released under an amnesty in 1898.

Clarke issued his own death warrant on 23 April 1916, in the form of the first and only issue of words "The Irish Republic" and was released in Dublin to announce the Sinn Fein Easter uprising: "The following have been named as the Provisional Government:- Thomas J. Clarke ..." His was the first of seven names. Two thousand rebels held the centre of the city for a week.

Martyrdom came for Clarke on 3 August 1916.

Common land – Portland's commons have a right of public access, on foot, "for air and exercise", given under section 193 of the Law of Property Act [1925] which applies to all common land inside the pre-1974 boundaries of a borough or urban district. Portland has many remnants of mediaeval common land that were registered in accordance with the Commons Registration Act [1965]:

CL2 – four miles of the Chesil Beach from the Bound Stone on the parish boundary with Chickerell (SY 644 775) south to include Chesil Cove and end beneath West Weares (SY 683 729). The same registration includes a separate small area of common land on the cliffside beneath Bower's Quarries (SY 681 720) and resumes below Grangecroft Quarries (SY 679 709) as a continuous strip which expands across the whole of the unenclosed part of Portland Bill – going up to and around the fence of the Underwater Weapons Establishment – and extending around the eastern coast to Cave Hole (SY 687 691). It resumes again above Cheyne Weare and the Southwell Landslip (SY 694 706) in a strip along the east side of Southwell Road. After another break there is a further part of this common around Church Hope Cove (SY 697 710). A southern offshoot from the Cave Hole section is The Butts which is the mediaeval archery range, from the cliff at the Battery above Red Pools (SY 683 688) inland for 400 yards to the road at Harpland, north-east of the Lower Lighthouse (SY 682 691), on the west side of public footpath number 46. Lastly, in the centre of the southern part of the island, there is a tiny vestige of common land beside Porrick's Lane at Sweet Hill, Southwell (SY 685 699).

CL4 – Verne Yeates, along the top of the hill above Fortuneswell, from Priory Corner (SY 685 729) to the ditch of the Verne Prison (SY 694 733) and including the viewpoint car-park.

CL71 – the isthmus from the Chesil Beach north to Small Mouth, beside the dismantled railway line (SY 668 761).

CL72 – the verge of Wide Street, Easton (SY 687 726) and all other bits of roadside grass south to Weston Green (SY 686 712) and Weston Pond (SY 686 710).

Conjuror's Lodge – nickname for the former chapel on the corner of Clements Lane, Chiswell. It was established by a breakaway sect who were thrown out of the Methodist community for allegedly believing in witchcraft [1816]. It was reached by an external staircase, with a store beneath. Religious use ceased after only a decade [1826].

Convicts – see entries for **Portland convict poem**, **Forger's Slate**, **Portland Harbour**, **Verne Citadel**, and the **Young Offenders' Institution**.

Convict Prison: austere Victorian views of the buildings in The Grove.

Coode – eminent civil engineer **Sir John Coode** [1816-92] established his reputation by taking over the building of Portland Harbour on the death of its designer, James

Meadows Rendel, and persevering as Engineer-in-Chief until its first stage was completed [1856-72].

It earned him a knighthood [1872], on completion of the Inner and Outer Breakwaters, and a commission from the colonial government in South Africa for a similar "Harbour of Refuge" in Table Bay, Capetown.

His harbours are dotted across the globe from Waterford in Ireland and Dover, England, to Colombo, Ceylon, and Portland (Victoria) and Fremantle in Australia.

Court Leet – enforcement of the rights, dues and practices of the Royal Manor of Portland, including control of its commonable lands, is vested in this body. It meets twice a year and comprises 24 jurymen and a foreman, elected by the tenants and owners of properties on the manor. Various of its customs dated from Saxon times, including until its abolition in the Victorian era the use of a reeve staff to record the manorial plots and the payment of rents.

This was an annual quite-rent, at 3d per acre, collected by an official of the court who was known as the Reeve. He was appointed at the Michaelmas Court and would be the tenant who had paid the highest amount of quit-rent but had not held office before. No person could hold the appointment twice.

The total amount the court has to pay to the sovereign is £14.14s.3d. This was never increased for inflation though £1, which also became a token sum, was retained towards payment of the Reeve. Rents climbed slightly higher than the dues, to £15.5s.8d. in 1875.

The Michaelmas Court used to be held at Weston and was followed by dinner, of broccoli and artichokes, at The Lugger, which had the distinction of being the first building on Portland with glass windows. Then the meeting place moved to the nearby George Inn.

Reeve staffs are displayed at Portland Museum but the most precious, in silver from the ducat treasure of a Spanish galleon shipwrecked on Portland, "was presented to Queen Victoria as Lady of the Manor".

Courting customs – mainlanders who came to Portland because of the stone trade were surprised to find the islanders almost a separate breed; a race of natives clinging to a code of morals long forgotten elsewhere.

Their marriage customs are quaintly divulged by a London printer in a manner which, although outwardly in the style of the late 18th century, comes near to a modern mass newspaper or sociological study in its approach. This account I wrote under the name Ross Brown for an early issue of Dorset County Magazine in 1968 – when pseudonyms disguised a lack of contributors.

John Smeaton, builder of the third Eddystone lighthouse, completed in 1759, visited the quarries of Portland and had as guide a Mr

Roper. He told Smeaton of a local love custom which ensures compatibility by not allowing marriage until the girl is pregnant.

Though the custom sounds to be too close to free love to have been the basis for morality, in a closed society highly coloured by tradition, I am sure that Portland is unique only in being the example which was recorded. Certainly the withdrawn and inbred nature of the place helped the way of life from another age to survive intact. Similarities exist with the then current American practice of bundling and before the imposition of moral ethics this must have been habitual everywhere. "Portland custom" it was called – which is shorter than attempting the explanation in current phraseology.

Smeaton admired the strength and healthy looks of the Portland men, and the ease with which they operated in the quarries. He asked Roper where "they could possibly pick up such a set of stout hardy fellows". Roper: If you knew how these men are produced you would wonder the less for all our marriages are productive of children.

Smeaton: Can you give an explanation of how this happens?

R: Our people here, as they are bred up to hard labour, are very early in a condition to marry and provide a family. They intermarry with one another, very rarely going to the mainland to seek a wife and it has been the custom of the Isle, from time immemorial, that they never marry till the woman is pregnant.

S: But pray, does not this subject you to a great number of bastards? Have not your Portlanders the same kind of fickleness in their attachments, that Englishmen are subject to and in consequence, does not this produce many inconveniences?

R: None at all, for previous to my arrival here, there was but one child on record of the parish register, that had been born a bastard, in the compass of 150 yards. The mode of courtship here is that a young woman never admits of the serious addresses of a young man, but on the supposition of a thorough probation. When she becomes with child, she tells her mother; the mother tells her father; and he tells the boy, that is then the proper time to be married.

S: But suppose, Mr Roper, she does not prove with child, what happens then – do they live together without marriage, or, if they separate, is not this such an imputation upon her, as to prevent her getting another suitor?

R: The case is thus managed. If the woman does not prove with a child, after a competent time of courtship, they conclude they are not destined by providence for each other: they therefore separate; and as it is an established maxim, which the

Portland women observe with great strictness, never to admit to plurality of lovers at one time, their honour is no-ways tarnished. She just as soon (after the affair is declared to be broke off) gets another suitor, as if she had been left a widow, or that nothing had ever happened, but that she remained a virgin.

S: But pray, sir, did nothing particular happen upon your men coming down from London?

R: Yes, our men were much struck, and mightily pleased, with the facility of the Portland ladies; and it was not long before several of the women proved with child: but the men being called upon to marry them, this part of the lesson they were uninstructed in. On their refusal, the Portland women arose to stone them out of the Isle: inso much that those few who did not care to take their sweethearts for better, for worse, after so fair a trial were, in reality, obliged to decamp. On this occasion, one bastard only was born; but since then matters have gone according to the ancient custom.

Crystal – the acoustic calibration vessel moored in Portland Harbour, towards the Outer Breakwater. Operating as the offshore arm of the Admiralty Research Establishment she has lines unlike any other ship, resembling a row of terraced houses with few windows and a flat roof, rising to a tower block at one end. Outer and inner sides are sloping. Underwater she has a flat bottom.

D

D-Day – Dorset was the Concentration Area for the marshalling of men and materials for V United States Corps (Force O) of the first US Army which sailed for Omaha Beach, between Point du Hoe and Colleville on the Normandy coast, in Operation Overlord on the night of 5 June 1944.

This Corps comprised the 1st United States Infantry Division, the 2nd United States Infantry Division, the 2nd United States Armored Division and two Ranger Battalions. Commander-in-Chief of Allied land forces was General [later Field Marshal and Viscount] Bernard Law Montgomery [1887-1976],

V Corps, which lost 2,000 men on the bloodiest of the invasion beaches, sailed from Weymouth and Portland.

BUKO (West) was the Build Up Control Organisation for the First United States Army and the Second British Army, with headquarters at Portsmouth, and came under the control of Brigadier [later Major-General Sir] Gerald Duke [born 1910].

BUKO (East) was a bogus logistical operation set up in Dover to deceive the Germans into thinking the attack would come in the Calais area.

Part of the British 30 Corps (Force G) sailed for Gold Beach, Bayeux, from Poole Harbour. Ahead of them, however, were the gliders of the British 6th Airborne Division which had been towed into the sky from Tarrant Rushton before midnight on 5 June.

The first Allied soldiers to arrive in France on D-Day, 6 June 1944, were the 171 men carrying out Operation Coup de Main. Their six gliders landed near Benouville, to take the Orne River swing-bridge and the Orne Canal bridge, codenamed Pegasus. That was captured and held by Major John Howard with 'D' Company of the 2nd Battalion, Oxfordshire and Buckinghamshire Light Infantry. They had opened the Second Front in the European theatre of war.

The Dead House – the scale of shipwreck tragedies in Chesil Cove,

D-Day: embarkation from Castletown hards at Portland, for Omaha Beach.

the Deadman's Bay corner of the Chesil Beach at Chiswell, was such that a fish-store at the side of the pebble beach was set aside as a mortuary (SY 683 733). Drowned bodies were dragged to the Dead House, as it was known, to await their inquest and burial. Garage-size double doors open directly on to the beach.

Deadman's Bay – Thomas Hardy's name for the blandly mapped West Bay, plus Chesil Cove, off Chiswell (SY 680 734), in his novel *The Well-Beloved* [1892]. He was thinking, in particular, of the hundreds of bodies washed up after a gale wrecked Sir Hugh Cloberry Christian's fleet [1796].

Dramatic shipwrecks would continue into the 20th century and be compounded by the massacre by German E-boats of 638 Americans on their way to an invasion exercise at Slapton Sands, Devon [1944].

HMS *Delight* – 1,375-ton 'Defender' class destroyer dive-bombed and sunk by Junkers Ju.87 'Stukus' 20 miles south of Portland Bill [29 July 1940].

Shortly after she had gone down an intercepted German radio message machine-encrypted in the "Enigma" code was deciphered by the British Code and Cipher School, Bletchley Park, Hertfordshire. It stated that the warship "had been sunk with the aid of Freya reports". That, Air Ministry intelligence would confirm, meant that the Germans had established operational coastal radar stations, hastily set-up after their occupation of the Cherbourg peninsula – 71 miles south of Portland Bill.

Denham – poet and architect **Sir John Denham** [1615-69] travelled to see the quarries of Portland after the Great Fire of London [1666], in his capacity as the King's Surveyor General of Works, but was seized with a "distemper of madness".

John Aubrey says he "came within a mile of it, turned back to London again, and did not see it". It seems he turned back from the Small Mouth ferry crossing beside the Chesil Beach. Denham visited Charles II and told him he was the Holy Ghost. His deputy, Christopher Wren, took over the rebuilding of London.

Dough-cake – see entry for **Portland dough-cake**.

The *Dreadnought* Hoax – William Horace de Vere Cole [1881-1936], alias the man from the Foreign Office, and Miss Virginia Stephen, known to us as the writer Virginia Woolf [1882-1941], carried out one of the greatest practical jokes of all time in Portland Harbour [1910]. Fitted out by Clarkson's in suitable oriental costume, were alleged members of the Abyssinian royal family, who for the convenience of their interpreter spoke a mix of Swahili and Latin pronounced backwards.

They telegrammed HMS Dreadnought, lying off Portland, on 10 February. Or, rather, sent the message in the name of Sir Charles Hardinge [1858-1944], the Permanent Under Secretary for Foreign Affairs, who would later in the year be created first Baron Hardinge of Penshurst:

"COMMANDER-IN-CHIEF HOME FLEET PORTLAND STOP PRINCE MAKALENNIA AND SUITE ARRIVE FOUR-TWENTY TODAY WEYMOUTH STOP HE WISHES TO SEE DREADNOUGHT STOP KINDLY ARRANGE MEET THEM ON ARRIVAL STOP REGRET SHORT NOTICE STOP FORGOT WIRE BEFORE STOP INTERPRETER ACCOMPANIES STOP HARDINGE FOREIGN OFFICE STOP"

It was received by Admiral Sir William May [1849-1930], Commander-in-Chief of the Home

Fleet, at anchor in Portland Harbour, aboard his flagship HMS *Dreadnought*. The time was 3.45 in the afternoon and there was only half an hour in which to put on full dress, arrange for a guard of honour to be mounted on board, and send a launch to the jetty to meet the royal party.

Meanwhile, they were being met off the London train by the town's civic dignitaries, the Mayor and Corporation of Weymouth, and ushered into "a four-wheeler" and a taxicab for the short drive to the harbourside. Willie Clarkson had fitted them out magnificently, the Daily Mirror reported:

"All the princes wore vari-coloured silk sashes as turbans, set off with diamond aigrettes, white gibbah tunics, over which were cast rich flowing robes, and round their necks were suspended gold chains and jewelled necklaces.

"Their faces were coloured a deep brown with a specially-prepared powder, and half-hidden under dark false beards and moustaches, while, except in the case of the lady, their hair was dyed black and crisply curled.

"The young lady's make up – she is described as very good looking, with classical features – was precisely the same as that of the other princes, save that her long hair was bound up tightly on the top of her head, and she also wore a black curly wig.

"They also all wore patent leather boots which, Oriental fashion, tapered to a point, the ends projecting fully six inches beyond the toes.

"White gloves covered the princes' hands, and over the gloved fingers they wore gold wedding-rings – heavy plain circlets, which looked very impressive.

"Prince Makalen, as chief of the royal party, had an additional ornament. This was the real Imperial Order of Ethiopia – a star-shaped jewel, in the centre of which was a sapphire-like piece of glass. It was suspended from a red, gold and blue ribbon, and was pinned on – with a safety-pin – to a gold chain worn round the neck. The metal was of Abbysinian silver plated with gold. The total value of the jewellery worn by the princes was at least £500."

Stepping out of the Admiral's launch and climbing the gangplank of the battleship they were piped aboard and welcomed to the strains of the Zanzibar national anthem, which was the closest tune the band could attempt, "not knowing that of Abyssinia, if such a thing exists".

First up the gangway was Horace de Vere Cole, purporting to be Herbert Cholmondely, the Foreign Office Attaché. He shook hands with Admiral May. Then came the princes – Prince Makalen, Prince Sanganya, then Prince Mandok and

Prince Mikael Golen. Prince Sanganya was in fact a young lady, known to us as Virginia Woolf. The others were Duncan Grant, Anthony Buxton and Guy Ridley. They were formally introduced to Admiral May and then to Captain Herbert W. Richmond, the chief officer of the *Dreadnought.*

The princes then inspected the guard of honour of the Royal Marines. Prince Makalen was talking gibberish. "Yembo inscara milu berrango scutala bonga asterma el crashbi shemal," was an approximation of one of his utterances.

Herr George Kauffman had come with the part and was, said Cholmondely, a German who was acting as the official interpreter. He was Adrian Stephen, Virginia's brother, disguised by beard and bowler. "The Prince wishes to know," said Kauffman, "the difference between the red and blue marines."

The explanation was provided and duly translated by Kauffman into gibberish for the benefit of Prince Makalen.

The question of a salute was raised. Eighteen guns was suggested by naval officers who were embarrassed that they had no Abyssinian flag to hoist as it was fired. Kauffman relayed the British regret to the princes who gracefully accepted the apology and said they would waive any claim to a salute.

As they proceeded around the entire ship, with everything being shown to them and explained via Herr Kauffman, the princes "alternately beamed with pleasure and glared ferociously".

Cholmondely, acting as the man from the Foreign Office, went below with a group of officers to take tea. He explained the family's relationship with the chief. Next day, he added, the princes intended travelling to Eton to make arrangements for sending their sons and nephews to school in England.

He was taken to task about the short notice that was given of the impending visit. "We ourselves had only a matter of hours in which to arrange things," Cholmondely explained. "The party was visiting France but had to be rushed away suddenly from Paris in order to escape the floods. The Seine is still rising, apparently."

Admiral May then came down to ask Mr Cholmondely if he could be of further service. He was thanked for his courtesy and kindness and told that the princes, Mr Cholmondely was sure, would excuse him from further ceremony. The Admiral departed to disrobe and put on mufti to go ashore.

The royal party had then to make their excuses, saying they had already eaten far too much that day, in order to avoid drinking tea – being "afraid that the least moisture would remove the powder from their skin".

They were now making their goodbyes but the Flag Officer insisted on accompanying the party to the jetty at Weymouth Harbour. As they left the *Dreadnought,* walking down the gangway, the long pointed boots nearly caused the downfall of one of the princes and the exposure of the sham: "He slipped on a step and would have fallen into the sea had not one of his royal confreres caught him by the arm and saved him from an untimely ducking, to say nothing of the exposure of the hoax that would have followed."

The band had again struck up the Zanzibar national anthem. Two official motor cars were waiting for the party at the harbour. Here the chief Prince of Abyssinia, Prince Makalen, was so overwhelmed with the warmth of their reception that he conveyed to the Flag-Lieutenant his wish to present to him the Imperial Order of Ethiopia.

The young officer declined, saying that he would not accept or wear a foreign order without special permission, but that he was deeply touched by the kind thought.

On the return train, the masquerade was maintained, with Cholmondely telling Great Western Railway officials that the princes could not eat any meals that had been served with the naked hand. Miss Stephen told the Daily Mirror:

"There were no spare gloves on the train, and the officials subsequently had to buy a few pairs, grey kid gloves. We gave them princely tips."

Prince Sanganya's story appeared in the Daily Mirror of 15 February 1910. Virginia Stephen was asked how difficult it had been to pose as a man.

"I spoke as little as possible in case my voice, which I made as gruff as I could, should fail me. I found I could easily laugh like a man, but it was difficult to disguise the speaking voice.

"As a matter of fact the only really trying time I had was when I had to shake hands with my first cousin, who is an officer on the *Dreadnought,* and who saluted me as I went on deck. I thought I should burst out laughing, but happily, I managed to preserve my Oriental stolidity of countenance."

Her cousin was Captain Willy Fisher, who became Admiral Sir William Wordsworth Fisher [1875-1937]. "He took it to heart a great deal," in Virginia's words, and for the rest of his life avoided seeing her again. Unlike the two Herberts in the story.

Herbert would meet Herbert again in the days that followed the hoax. On the Sunday afternoon, in the West End, Captain Herbert Richmond of HMS *Dreadnought* came face to face with Horace de Vere Cole, alias Herbert Cholmondely of the Foreign Office.

They smiled and shook hands, and the captain was also reunited with Herr Kauffman, the German interpreter, now sans fiery moustache and whiskers.

"It was very cleverly done," Captain Richmond said, admitting that the audacious trick had deceived them completely. The officers had no idea at the time that a practical joke was being played on them and later, when they learned they had been hoaxed, they laughed heartily.

Press interest had now become insatiable and Admiral May sensibly took the *Dreadnought* to sea and waited for the joke to die down. "Bunga-bunga" had become the local form of address for her sailors, and Pavilion music-hall comedian Medly Barrett opened his act with a doggerel verse to the tune of *The Girl I Left Behind Me:*

When I went on board a Dreadnought *ship,*
Though I looked just like a costermonger
They said I was an Abyssinian prince,
Because I shouted "Bunga-bunga".

Miss Stephen, as herself, was already a frequent visitor to the Dorset coast. She had holidayed with Clive and Vanessa Bell and Walter Lamb in rented cottages at Studland in the second half of September 1909. They returned to Harbour View, Studland, on 26 March 1910, after the *Dreadnought* hoax, and she did not return to 29 Fitzroy Square until 16 April 1910.

It is now on April Fools Day that the incident is widely recalled.

E

Easton – The central village of the Portland toplands radiating from Edwardian municipal gardens at Easton Square (SY 691 719). These were opened by Councillor H. Sansom in April 1904.

Easton Street leads north, carrying the island's eastern main road, with the notable building being No.28, on the east side, beside the entrance to Loves Croft. "1760 WILLIAM PEARCE AND REBECCA HIS WIFE BUILDED THIS HOUSE," an inscription proclaims on the first-floor fireplace. Columns and mouldings proclaim a building of style.

The New Inn, on the west side, dates from the late 18th century. Palmers Croft lies behind.

Eastwards from Easton Square is Straits. Southwards is Park Lane cul-de-sac. Westwards is Reforne. All have a selection of older buildings.

Religion arrived with a Wesleyan Chapel [1854], followed by the Anglican All Saints [1916], and a Salvation Army Hall [1926].

Easton Gardens – laid out in 1904, among the houses at the centre of Portland's top-lands (SY 692 718) these have been stripped of all of what Stuart Morris called "Edwardian elegance". They lost railings, bandstand and trees to a bland suburban mediocrity.

Easton Pond Massacre – in the evening of the first Saturday of April 1803 a naval pressgang of about 60 marines and sailors landed by Portland Castle, from the *Eagle* frigate anchored in Portland Roads. They raided Chiswell village, beside the Chesil Bank, and took away Henry Wiggot and Richard Way. Other villagers fled on to the top of the island and made a stand at Easton Pond, in Easton Square (SY 692 718).

The captain of the pressgang grabbed a man by the collar. He pulled back and the captain fired his pistol.

The marines took this as a signal to fire into the crowd and three Portlanders fell dead. They were Richard Flann (aged 42), A. Andrews (47) and William Lano. Each had been shot through the head. The first two were quarrymen, and all three were married. Lano, a blacksmith, was at the door of his shop. Another man was shot through the thigh and a young woman through the back.

An inquest returned verdicts of "Wilful murder".

Ebenezer – the ship that achieved a unique claim to fame, having sailed up the English Channel without passing south of Portland Bill. Instead the 95-ton sailing vessel, a government sloop carrying stores for the Royal Navy, was left stranded on top of the Chesil Beach by "the great gale" [23 November 1824].

She was later tugged down the unstable pebble bank and relaunched at high tide into a specially dug trench that saw her safely seaworthy in Portland Roads. She resumed her voyage, from Plymouth to Portsmouth.

Edward – it was as **King Edward VIII** [1894-1972] that he visited Portland [12 November 1936] to review forty ships of the Home Fleet. This was to be his first and last visit to the fleet as monarch and his train arrived at Portland to an inauspiciously wild reception. The train pulled into the station yard just before 4.30am in a full gale.

A wave had broken over the Chesil Beach and flooded Victoria Square and Castletown, and across the station yard where there was two feet of water beneath the royal train. The King remained sleeping, however, until eight o'clock. The royal car had to force its way between floodwater and cheering children on its route to the dockyard.

He embarked on the royal yacht *Victoria and Albert* to cross the turbulent waters to the warships straining at anchor.

A 21-gun salute crashed across the water as the sun broke through. The King's inspection was undertaken in the Commander-in-Chief's barge, and he then lunched on the flagship *Nelson*.

In the evening he attended a concert party given aboard HMS *Courageous*, followed by dinner on the Royal Yacht. The following afternoon thousands of people lined the streets of Weymouth as the King drove to the main station to board a train for Paddington. This time the sun shone and he was given an enthusiastic send off.

A month later he abdicated.

Ehen – French barque, sailing from Bordeaux to Bremen, wrecked on the rocks at Portland Bill [31 October 1890]. The wind was light and the crew and passengers reached shore safely, in their own boats.

Elena R. – Greek steamship sunk by a German mine off the Shambles sandbank, Portland [22 November 1939].

Epitaphs – as might be expected of the country's best quarriers, Portlanders were expressive in their gravestones. Epitaphs are common, and often some humour is put into the mouths of the dead, though the stones in the old parish churchyard of St Andrew's (SY 697 711) have taken a mauling from landslips and history.

Andrew Stone, whose stone gives his death as 30 July 1764, reminds one of the inevitable: "Remember me as thou pass by. As thou art now, so once was I, and as I am now, so you must be. Prepare yourself to follow me."

Susannah Comben, daughter of Silas and Elizabeth Comben, died on 22 June 1737, aged 31: "My friends and lover left behind, I pray for me no longer weep. I am espoused to Christ in Heaven with God, my marriage day to keep." Remarked the Portland Year Book in 1905. "Susannah, who was a lover at the age of 31, would be shocked did she live in these degenerate days, when girls are lovers at 13 and lads at 14."

Poor Abel Pearce died young, and consequently missed a number of opportunities for enjoying sin: "Grieve not for me nor be sad. The shorter time I live the fewer sins I had."

One, however, was able to reconcile virtue with age: "In memory of Edward Pearce, Superintendent of His Majesty's Quarries, who died 19 June, 1745, aged 58. I never did a slander forge, My neighbour's fame to wound, Nor hearken to a false report, By malice whispered round."

Abel Flew, who was buried on 25 October 1676, worked and lived for stone, and saw it as unavoidable that when the day of the resurrection came, he would be back with the old product again: "In life I wroath in stone, Now life is gone I know I shall be raised, By a stone an By such a stone as giveth living breath and saveth The Righteous from the Second death."

A gravestone at St George's gives a straight piece of history: "Sacred to the memory of William Hansford, aged 64 years, who was killed on the 23 November 1824 by the sea overflowing the village of Chissel. His leg was broken in attempting to make his escape. Afterwards the house fell on him." No eulogy for him, just concise, accurate reporting.

Everleigh – 5,222-ton cargo ship outward bound down the English Channel, for New York, torpedoed and sunk off Dorset by German submarine *U-1017* [6 February 1945].

Exercise Tiger – the Slapton Sands practice for D-Day that went disastrously wrong and left Castletown Pier, Portland, piled high with the corpses of hundreds of American GIs.

See the entries for ***LST507*** and ***LST531***, and that for the **Slapton Sands Massacre**.

F

Floating Dock – formerly in Portland Harbour, moored between the Dock Jetty and Coaling Pier (SY 693 748) for repair and refitting of escort vessels and submarines [from 1922]. In use during and after the Second World War, being known to the Royal Navy as Auxiliary Floating Dock 19, until such work was concentrated at Devonport [1959].

Flood disasters – on 13 February 1979 the sea surged across the top of the Chesil Beach and swept hundreds of tons of shingle, and several parked cars, along with it in a swirling surf that left Victoria Square flooded to a depth of four feet. The water came over the pebble bank above the Masonic Hall.

It had already come through the pebbles in a less dramatic fashion earlier that winter, in December 1978, and each time completely cut the road link with the mainland. Both times the lower parts of Chiswell were inundated and but for the benefit of Portland's geology, the fact that the tightly-packed homes are constructed in one of the best building stones of these islands, house collapses would have occurred. In the event the navy came to the rescue with helicopters and Zodiac inflatables.

Flood disasters: waves break across the Chesil Beach in 1979.

What mystified the emergency services about the spectacular events of 13 February 1979 was that no one predicted them, and though atmospheric pressure was low (which allows sea levels to rise) the wind was a light easterly, the opposite direction from the south-westerly waves. There was neither an extreme local storm nor the forecast of an exceptionally high tide.

One view is that the freak wave, which was six feet higher than the Chesil Beach, was a trumani caused by an earthquake on the mid-Atlantic tectonic divide. Such pressure waves are carried through the entire volume of the ocean seas but become magnified on reaching the shallow waters of the coast.

An earlier "tidal wave", almost certainly caused by an oceanic earthquake rather than the weather, occurred on 19 August 1763. The sea suddenly rose by ten feet "and then retired instantly".

The 1979 puzzle is the subject of an article in the journal *Weather* [November 1983] which claims that subsequent examination of meteorological data found another possible culprit for the Portland disaster. It was a deep but dying depression 2,000 miles away to the south-west in mid-Atlantic, and Portland's problem took 48 hours to reach the Dorset coast. An automatic buoy beyond the Scillies recorded waves that were of normal proportions from this kind of storm but had crests abnormally far apart. Their arrival off Dorset coincided with the high tide and low pressure; the sea level was already a metre higher than that predicted for high water in the tide tables.

On top of this full sea the long waves had a clear run up the Southwest Approaches and were set to hit the great shingle bank at Chiswell frontally at 90 degrees. In places they had no difficulty sweeping over the top of the bank, managing two metres of water across at a time with a force that

Ferrybridge crossing: beside Portland Harbour, from the air and the shore of Small Mouth.

maintained the wave form on its initial descent down the pebbles into the streets and homes. The flooding is therefore put down to a combination of unlikely factors, which current monitoring systems could not forecast, and there is no guess at a time scale for the probability of a repeat.

Portlanders are a resilient breed and realise that it has all happened before. There was 1824 – which virtually destroyed the old Fleet parish church – and its repeat performance in 1942.

Shortly after 11.00 hours on 13 December, a Sunday morning, in 1942 the water began to seep through the great wall of pebbles. At midday the first waves poured over the top; and within a short time the slight layer of water across Victoria Square had risen to over five feet. To quote a reporter: "At one stage only an inch or two of the letter box in Victoria Square was showing above the flood and letters floated out on the tide."

The stout stone wall which runs beside the beach road was reduced to rubble at many points and the railway line was breached for several yards, sleepers were swept away and rails buckled. The water put the island's gasworks out of action for 36 hours and a trail of mud, clay, shingle and boulders were strewn across the low-lying part of Chiswell when the sea receded.

The first buildings to be flooded had been the remains of houses on the west side of Chiswell and Big Ope. These had been reduced to ruins by the flood of 1824 and many were never repaired. Some have now been converted into workshops, or cleared away in the making of the esplanade, but others can still be seen today.

R. Flann of 109 Big Ope told reporters that many people had put flood-boards to their doors when the sea started seeping through the Chesil Beach. But the tide had "pitched off" and everyone was surprised when the first waves came over the bank. He continued:

"I had just got into the Cove House Inn, which is on the highest part of the beach. There wasn't much of a wind blowing although the south-south-easterly storms had been piling up the water in the bay. The sea was making a terrific roar as huge ground swells swept up the beach. Then I heard an even louder roar and the sea hit the side of the house.

"It must have been 60 feet high. The front door of the inn was shut but the wave rushed through the window and caught me square in the chest. I was thrown up against the bar, but I got away with only a cut on the back of my hand. I was lucky; I have never seen such waves in my life."

The Comben family, the landlords of the inn, took refuge upstairs.

They came down three hours later to find the till filled with water, windows smashed, and glasses and cigarettes swept from the shelves. The frontage to the inn was washed away and the Combens spent the afternoon clearing up the mess. At seven o'clock punctually the inn opened again.

Mr J. Galpin, a fisherman of Three Yard Close, saw the waves hit the Cove House Inn and watched water pour down the roof and walls. He commented: "The people who built that place must have known what they were about.

"I was on the cliffs watching. Chiswell was covered in a cloud of spray. I saw the first great wave come rushing across the bay. A two-ton logwood which came out of the old *Rand*, a sailing ship wrecked many years ago, was picked up like a straw. The logwood smashed into my hut, which contained five tons of old iron saws, and took it through a stone wall as if it had never been there. The remains of the hut were thrown down several yards away.

"An old boat was swept over three six-foot walls right out into the road a hundred yards away. The hut, as you can see, is just matchwood. All my gear was inside and everything I get my living with is gone, except my boat, which I had taken to a safe place."

One of the homeless was 75-year-old Mr L. White who had gone to sea in sailing ships and remembered the wreck of the Norwegian barque *Christiana* at the end of the last century: "I was then washed out of another house on the beach. But it wasn't as bad as this. There hasn't been such a bad day since 120 years ago, when a lot of people were drowned."

Mr White was told that his cottage, in a little alley close to the beach, would have to be demolished. Silt and yellow clay was a foot deep on the floor and the water had covered his coal fire which went out in a cloud of steam. All his clothes were ruined and like many others he was helped by members of Portland Women's Voluntary Service who were soon on the spot with hot dinners, bedding and clothes. The relief operation was swift – Britain was at war and emergencies were expected.

National newspapers sensationalised the floods with stories that the Chesil Bank had been either "breached" or "washed away".

This worried a number of eminent geologists who took the reports at their face value and had visions of one of the greatest marvels of our landscape looking as if the dambusters (excuse the hindsight!) had been through it. Nothing of the kind had happened; the sea started by filtering through the 42-feet high bank and later came over the top as well. Some pebbles washed down in Chiswell but there is no evidence that the sea has ever torn through the Chesil Beach, though the waters have revealed its core of blue clay.

Folly Pier – known as the New Pier [1760] but soon renamed when its exposed position beneath the East Weares (SY 705 726), coupled with landward inaccessibility, quickly consigned it to history.

Forest – large fully-rigged Canadian sailing ship of 1,422-tons, so named "because it took a forest to build her". Constructed at Hantsport, and registered at Windsor, Nova Scotia, she sank off Portland Bill after a collision with the New Zealand emigre clipper *Avalanche*, which was also sailing home from London [11-12 September 1877].

The *Forest* had delivered timber to London and was returning empty, apart from minimal ballast, therefore being "high in the water".

Nine of her crew, including the master Ephraim Lockhart, aged 50, and his 33-year-old mater, Robert McValine, were saved. The other twelve were drowned.

Forger's Slate – now in Portland Museum, this is an elaborate tribute to a prison warder, etched like a printing plate by an engraver who was said to have lost his freedom for copying a banknote. It

is an intricate representation of the tomb with an even more elaborate border which carries the heading: "H. M. Convict Prison, Portland: Governor G. Clifton, Esq." Below the wheel of life is the ...

"Memorial of the late Chief Warder Brooks. Who, while on duty on 19th January 1881 was seized with apoplexy and, mid universal regret, expired in 36 hours.

"Sacred to the Memory of William Thomas Brooks. Born 14th August 1822. Died 21st January 1881.

"Now is the axe laid at the root of the tree. Watch therefore for ye know not the day nor the hour."

There was also official grief at his demise, with the governor recording:

"It is with no ordinary feeling of regret that I have to record the sudden death of my faithful chief warder, Mr W. T. Brooks from an attack of paralysis, brought on from exposure while on duty during the intensely cold weather which prevailed at the beginning of that month."

The medical officer added his words to the prison's annual report: "I regret also to record the death of chief warder W. Brooks from a very sudden attack of apoplexy; he was seized while standing by my side and talking to me; he was at once removed to the hospital, where he

HMS 'Formidable': her final photograph.

became rapidly worse and died in a few hours.

"The death caused the most profound regret, as [he was] held in the highest esteem alike by officers and prisoners."

HMS *Formidable* – sailing last in line with the Fifth Battle Squadron from Portland Harbour, she was torpedoed in Lyme Bay, off Lyme Regis by a German submarine [02.20 hours, 1 January 1915].

Her position was 20 miles east of Start Point. An orderly evacuation was carried out for two hours, as the 15,000-ton battleship appeared quite stable, but at 04.39 she slipped under quite suddenly.

U-boat *UB-24* was responsible, with two torpedoes from close range, and in the process only narrowly survived – having grazed the heaving keel of the 15,000-ton warship. Though the battleship floated for a couple of hours, deteriorating weather hampered escape and the rescue efforts.

Of the crew of 780, only 233 were saved, some in their own cutter

Fortuneswell streets: a prisoner's view, from Verne Citadel.

Fortuneswell details: rooftops from Verne Yeates, and looking up The Street in 1891.

which took twenty hours to reach the shore at Lyme Regis. The Brixham trawler *Provident* carried out heroic rescues, as did the escort cruisers HMS *Topaze* and *Diamond* which together brought a total of 80 survivors into Portland.

Fortuneswell – urban Portland on the steep slope beneath Verne Citadel (SY 685 735), eastwards to Chiswell and north to Castletown, perhaps best described as the "Street of Wells" in Thomas Hardy's *The Trumpet Major* [1880]:

"The steep incline before her was dotted with houses, showing the pleasant peculiarity of one man's doorstep behind his neighbour's chimney, and slabs of stone as the common material for walls, roof, floor, pig-sty, stable-manger, door-scraper, and garden-stile."

This description, of streets that became increasingly terraced and slate-roofed in Hardy's lifetime, was developed in *The Well-Beloved* [1892]:

"The towering rock, the houses above houses, one man's doorstep rising behind his neighbour's chimney, the gardens hung up by one edge to the sky, the vegetables growing on apparently almost vertical planes, the unity of the whole island as a solid and single block of limestone four miles long, were no longer familiar and commonplace ideas."

Fortuneswell as a name has an old pedigree, being first recorded as "Fortunes Well" [1608], taking its name from a belief in the occult star-telling powers of its water, in which one's luck could be seen.

Fossils – though at the heart of Dorset's Jurassic coast with its very stone comprising compressed shells and mud from those warm-water seas, Portland lacked the conditions to preserve giant ammonites and dinosaur remains of the sort for which Lyme Regis and Charmouth are famous.

Portland produces other fossils in quantity with the best of the old collections being displayed in Portland Museum, often after the pick of the crop had been purloined by the Governor of the Convict Prison for his personal collection, later displayed beside the offices of the Bath and Portland Stone Company.

Fossil Tree – the notable survivor of the island's Victorian fossil collection, initially gathered around the Prison Governor's house in The Grove, now has the best view on the island. It stands beside the car-park at Portland Heights Hotel (SY 688 729).

HMS *Foylebank* – anti-aircraft auxiliary, converted from a civilian steamship, sunk in Portland Harbour at the height of the Battle of Britain [4 July 1940]. Daylight dive-bombers left 60 dead in her burning wreckage, including Leading Seaman Jack Mantle who stuck to his pom-pom, firing at the Junkers Ju.87 "Stukas" as he and the ship were torn apart. He would be posthumously awarded the Victoria Cross – the first to be won by the Royal Navy from an action inside British territorial waters.

Freeman's Incline – see entry for **Merchants' Railway**.

G

Fossil Tree: stands beside Portland Heights Hotel.

Gavelkind – the sub-mediaeval system of property inheritance, distinguished by equal division amongst heirs, was perpetuated by Portlanders. It had its origin in Anglo-Saxon land tenure and also enshrined the right of the youngest son to inherit the tenancy to the original family homestead.

Such division of freeholds and other rights was encouraged and sustained on Portland by the potential high values of land which might one day be worked for stone. It was also invoked in the passing down of less lucrative assets, such as the pews in St George's Church, where ownerships ended up hopelessly sub-divided and entangled.

Gee – Portland spy **Ethel** (**Bunty**) **Gee**, who worked in the Admiralty records office, who would be arrested with fellow spy Harry Houghton and their Soviet control, Gordon Lonsdale, outside the Old Vic theatre in London [7 January 1961].

Beneath the groceries, Gee's shopping basket contained a film showing the construction of the nuclear submarine HMS *Dreadnought*, photographs of Admiralty documents, and a microfilm containing a further 310 shots of classified material. She would be sentenced to 15 years.

The source of high-grade operational information concerning the *Dreadnought* would never be traced.

George Inn – at the west end of Reforne, Portland (SY 688 719), is older than its 1765 datestone. Probably that was when the original building of about 1700 was extended upwards to give lofty ceiling heights. A window from the earlier period has chamfered stone mullions. In Victorian times this became the meeting place of the island's ancient Court Leet.

Gertrude – steamship, bound for Rotterdam, which ran into Blacknor [26 August 1894]. Her bows lifted into the air and the stern sank from sight, with the funnel just visible amidships. She was carrying iron pyrites, from Huelva, and fog was blamed for her loss. There was no wind and the 20 crew and passengers were saved.

Gibraltar of Wessex – Thomas Hardy's word picture of Portland, which features as the Isle of Slingers in his novel *The Well-Beloved* [1892]. The disguise is paper thin because he goes on to write of it being "connected to the mainland by a long thin neck of pebbles". It is a "singular peninsula ... carved by Time out of single stone ... that stretches out like the head of a bird into the English Channel."

Man had then taken over from nature, or rather the kimberlins had – particularly the convict sort – for outsiders from the mainland carved the replica Gibraltar out of Dorset's grey, outstretched foot.

HMS *Goodson* – a Royal Navy escort frigate, towed into Portland with irreparable damage after being torpedoed by German submarine *U-984* [24 June 1944].

Great Storm – a thousand men drowned off Portland on the evening of 16 November 1795 when their voyage from Spithead to the Caribbean failed to proceed beyond Bridport as the wind became a hurricane. It was the fleet of Rear-Admiral [Sir] Hugh Clobbery Christian [1747-98], newly appointed Commander-in-Chief West Indies, whose flagship, the 98-gun *Prince George*, limped back to Portsmouth with her rigging smashed and unseaworthy almost beyond repair.

The less fortunate craft foundered or were driven ashore. Two hundred bodies were picked up along the Chesil Beach.

The doomed vessels, including the *Golden Grove* from which just a single soul would be saved, were trapped in Deadman's Bay, as the locals call the Chesil Cove seaward of Chiswell where the pebbles of Chesil Beach extend in one direction and the rocks of Portland take over on the other.

H

Harbour – see entry for **Portland Harbour**.

Hardy – novelist and poet **Thomas Hardy** [1840-1928] featured Portland in many of his works. It provides virtually the entire setting for the novel *The Well-Beloved* [1892-97] and a remarkable poem *The Souls of the Slain* [1899] in which the spirits of soldiers killed in the South African War fly homeward over Portland Bill like migratory birds.

"The wild, herbless, weather-worn promontory" also provides the setting in *The Trumpet Major* [1880] for Anne Garland to watch HMS *Victory* sailing for Plymouth and Cape Trafalgar [1805], with Bob Loveday on board.

Harriers and the Kestrel – the first vertical landing by a fixed-wing aircraft on an aircraft-carrier took place when a prototype of Hawker Siddeley's project 1127 came down on HMS *Ark Royal* as she steamed at 5-knots east of The Shambles, Portland Bill [8 February 1963].

Alfred William (Bill) Bedford [born 1920], Hawker's chief test pilot, was at the controls of the jet that could hover – which led to it being called the Kestrel.

The Sea Harrier was developed from the P1127. It was found to take off with increased efficiency, at less speed, from ski-ramps rather than traditional flat decks. These appeared on the aircraft-carriers HMS *Invincible* [1978] and HMS *Hermes* [1979], and were incorporated in the next generation of ships, HMS *Illustrious* and the next *Ark Royal*, that were still being built.

The futuristic aircraft made its operational debut with the Fleet Air Arm at Yeovilton [19 September 1979] when 700A Naval Air Squadron was commissioned as the Sea Harrier Intensive Flying Trials Unit. Later 800, 801, and 899 Naval Air Squadrons were fitted out with Sea Harriers, as were a couple of RAF squadrons with their version of the aircraft, and most would be combat-ready and heading for the South Atlantic within a week of the Argentinian invasion of the Falkland Islands [2 April 1982].

HMS ***Hazard*** – Portland's submarine depot ship, sunk in a collision, with the hospital ship SS *Western Australia* [28 January 1918]. She was at least able to tend the surviving casualties.

Henchman – bishop **Humphrey Henchman** [1592-1675] was rector of Portland until the Civil War [1643]. His rectory and library on the island were destroyed by the

Parliamentarians and he withdrew to live at the Close, Salisbury, from where he maintained a secret correspondence with royalist leaders.

He would be largely responsible for the successful last leg of Charles II's escape from England after the Battle of Worcester [1651]. Having looked after the defeated monarch at Hele House, near Salisbury, he escorted him "on foot to Clarendon Park corner where he took horse with Colonel Philip, and proceeded to Hambledon, in Hampshire, and thence to Brighthelmstone, where a barque had been provided to carry him to France".

Rewards after the Restoration included appointment as Bishop of Salisbury [1660] and then the see of London, as Lord High Almoner [1663]. Dying wealthy, he left £767 to St Paul's Cathedral, which had been destroyed in the Great Fire [1666].

Hickory – diesel-powered civilian vessel sunk by a German mine off Portland [22 October 1940].

High Angle Battery – main late-Victorian artillery defences on Portland for the sea-lanes across Weymouth Bay and into Portland Harbour. Fifteen huge rifled muzzle-loaded cannon were mounted in barbettes set deeply into the stone plateau south of Verne Citadel with the guns elevated steeply in order to have a trajectory over the ground to the east (SY 694 733). Built in 1892 with two datestones for the Queen, Victoria Regina, over tunnels that led to underground shell and cartridge stores which were kept separate, several hundred yards apart, to minimise the danger of accidental explosion.

Narrow gauge railway lines go into the tunnels and around the rear of the barbettes. The guns comprise six 9-inch (range 5 miles), two $12^1/_2$-inch (range 4 miles), one 9-inch (range 3 miles), one 8-inch (range $2^1/_2$ miles), five 7-inch (range 2 miles). All were designed to fire Palliser-type shells into the first generation of ironclad battleships.

The gun barrels and the elaborate carriages and elevating gear, each combination of which weighed upwards of 20-tons, were sold for scrap in 1910. The gun emplacements and some ancillary buildings, such as side-arms stores, survived to become an ancient monument and were restored as a community project [1984].

Higher or **Upper Lighthouse** – as with the other former lighthouse, the one that is now Portland Bird Observatory, this was erected in 1716 and pulled down and rebuilt in 1869 (SY 677 693). It was sold by Trinity House when the present lighthouse became operational on

Portland Bill [1906] and became the home of Dr Marie Stopes, the founder of London's first family planning clinic, in 1929. Her second husband was Humphrey Verdon Roe, the co-founder of the Avro planemaking company.

Known also as Branscombe Lodge.

Hill-fort – the buildings of the huge Verne Citadel in 1860 accounted for the entrenchments of an Iron Age hill-fort. These may not have been on any great scale, but size would not have been all-important in such a perfect strategic position. Sheer rock-faces and unclimbable slopes would have protected three of its four sides.

Facing the level south-eastern approaches, however, the fort had double ramparts. John Aubrey, the antiquary, recorded them in the 1680s: "In the Isle of Portland is a double-worked camp, i.e. British."

Dorset's historian John Hutchins called the work "Danish" and claimed a trench from it extended "to every accessible part of the island", but he was corrected by Dr Herbert Lilley who wrote in 1883: "This entrenchment is ancient British, and is only seen on Verne Hill."

HMS *Hood* – the scuttled battleship of Portland Harbour. Portland's value as a harbour of refuge for the Channel Squadron of the Home Fleet at the outbreak of the First World War was put in peril

Higher Lighthouse: also known as the Upper Lighthouse.

by the lethal capacity of German submarines. The great fear of the Admiralty was that a U-boat would slip into one of the major Fleet bases and run amok with torpedoes. With such large, stationary targets, at exceptionally close range, the results could have been devastating. If there had been a "Pearl Harbour" style raid during the Great War it would have been carried out by submersibles, not aircraft.

It was with a sense of urgency and emergency that navy boffins attempted a solution to the problems of access into Portland Harbour. With four square miles of enclosed water it is the largest man-made harbour in the world. The entrances were necessarily wide and deep to allow the passage of the largest capital ships in the world. Somehow, these had to be blockaded.

The first attempt was with thousands of small, round glass bulbs in small net cases. They were suspended on strands of piano wire and the idea was that they would "bob about", if a submarine touched them. By then, however, it would probably have been too late to react, and the chances of anyone noticing the difference between submarine "bobbing" and the natural wave actions were slim. The idea was soon dropped and the

HMS 'Hood': in October 1914, before being stripped and scuttled to block the Southern Ship Channel into Portland Harbour.

bulbs were adopted by fishermen to replace the old canvas buffs. Similar ones can be seen hanging in many waterside inns.

Next there were torpedo nets, hanging like curtains across the channels and suspended from "cats" (floats). Tom Pike, who was at Portland at the time, remembered this arrangement worked well enough for the northern and eastern entrances, but failed at the southern entrance. Here, the main tide flowed out from the harbour. Like curtains in the wind, the nets tended to run at an angle with the flowing water. Five-ton "clumps" (anchors) were attached to the bottom of the nets, and for a while it seemed this would hold them rigid.

However, the experts had reckoned without the immense quantities of rubbish that float away from a huge battle fleet. Tom Pike recalled the havoc caused by the jetsam: "The nets were clogged, and at full tide they naturally flattened with the stream and lay useless on the surface, despite their heavy anchors. It used to be said that you could walk on the nets when they were filled with gash."

Finally it was decided that there was no time for further experimentation. The southern entrance to Portland Harbour would be abandoned. It was of use in certain weather conditions as a short cut to the open sea, but the other two entrances were sufficient, and easier to control. The decision was to block the channel completely, with an obsolescent battleship.

Selected for scuttling was the redundant iron-clad *Hood*, 14,000-tons, and she went down on 4 November 1914. The intention was that she would be raised after the war, but salvage was never attempted and the hull and crushed superstructure of the battleship are still there today.

Tom Pike now takes up the story: "When the *Hood* was properly in position for 'Exercise Sink' the deliberate flooding began. But she was not going down fast enough to stay in position. To correct this shift a large hole was blown in her side, causing her to turn-turtle with her bilge keel showing above the surface at low water. No submarine could come through now, but neither could the silt and rubbish be flushed from the harbour.

"As an idea of the amount of mud that used to flow out through the southern entrance, I remember a bucket of water being taken from the harbour after a gale. It was allowed to stand for twelve hours, and then drained leaving an inch of sediment in the bottom. The whole harbour is lowered five feet as the tide falls, so great quantities of mud must have gone out through the southern entrance. When the tide returned it brought in clean water.

So I should think that the sinking of the *Hood* has caused a dirtier harbour.

"In about 1960 the situation changed and the masts, guns and funnels of the *Hood* were no longer capable of supporting her upside-down weight. They snapped, and the big whale-back of her hull sank from sight. She must now be lying on her gunwales.

"This in turn lead to a new problem, and whilst the *Hood* used to break the force of a southerly gale, the seas could now pour into the harbour. A long, heavy swell could sweep over her and across to the outer coaling arm of the inner harbour and made this area of the port untenable for ships to lie alongside. If this problem ever causes the southern entrance to be blocked complete, then I foresee all the pollution being forced northwards and its only outlet would be on to Weymouth beach."

Events in the First World War were to show that it had been wise to barricade the entrances into Portland Harbour. Intrepid submarine commanders on each side were soon to make headlines or lose their lives, or achieve both. British submarines successfully established a protective barrier for the defence of the Expeditionary Force as it was transported to Belgium and France. The British submarine *E-9* was able to torpedo and sink the German cruiser *Hela* in Heligoland Bight and escape pursuing German destroyers. She later managed to torpedo a German destroyer moving at high speed off the mouth of the Ems River. Equally, the German presence was also lethal and two weeks after the British cruiser *Pathfinder* had been put to the bottom of the North Sea by a submarine, the German boat *U-9* destroyed three British cruisers, the *Hogue*, *Aboukir* and *Cressy*, within minutes of each other off the Hook of Holland. This was perhaps the greatest single personal achievement of any submarine commander in the history of submarine warfare.

For the British battleship Formidable, entering waters off west Dorset and sailing eastward across Lyme Bay to shell the Belgium coast, the last moment came on New Year's Day in 1915 when two torpedoes blew up the ship and 500 men. In the light of these reversals it is easy to see why the British Home Fleet made a tactical retreat to the comparative distance of Scapa Flow in the Orkneys, and regarded Portland as a front-line operational base. Anywhere further up the Channel was regarded as suicidal for warships, in the same way as British North Sea submarines were also able to ensure the immobility of the German deep-seas fleet.

Hope – returning up-Channel to her home port of Amsterdam, having been trading, or more likely engaging in piracy, in the West Indies, the 350-ton, 30-gun treasure ship was wrecked on the Chesil Beach in "tempestuous weather" on the night of 16 January 1749. The mast snapped and crashed on to the beach, enabling the captain, Boii Cornelius, and his 73 hands to clamber to safety on the pebbles.

"Ship ashore" was the cry that spread at day-break through Portland, Weymouth and the villages. Her cargo, mostly in gold, was worth £50,000 – a fortune in the then value of money – and well over half of it was plundered by "a vast concourse" who pillaged the vessel "as soon as the reflux of the sea had made the ship accessible". They roughly pushed the crew aside and disregarded their faltering foreign accents: "No wreck. The goods ours. Bring it to we and we will pay for it."

By this they meant salvage money, but the hostile crowd grew to an estimated 4,000 people, who held the Chesil Beach for several days. They were organised by Augustin Elliott, a Portland labourer, who "was the muster-master, the treasurer, and divider of the prey amongst his plundering regiment".

They were eventually brought to a halt by three Justices of the Peace and an armed party which went on to carry out house-to-house searches and recover £25,000 for agents of the ship's owners. Elliott was put on trial at Dorchester on 15 July 1749 but acquitted by a sympathetic jury after a six-hour hearing.

The *Hope*'s anchor was recovered in 1985 and is now lying beside the Anchor Inn at Seatown, Chideock.

Houghton – Portland spy **Harry Houghton** drove a Renault Dauphine and came to the attention of the security service following a tip-off to Detective Constable Leonard Burt of Weymouth police [autumn 1959]. Operation Off-White, named for the colour of his car, monitored a series of train trips to London, on the first Saturday of each month. He would be arrested in the capital [7 January 1961].

He had met his Soviet control, Gordon Lonsdale, with fellow spy Bunty Gee, outside the Old Vic theatre. Among the many incriminating items found in Houghton's home was a Christmas card from Gee, carrying the message "OURS IS A DANGEROUS BUSINESS". Houghton would be sentenced to 15 years.

Housman's convict – the realities of a Portland convict's life interrupt the rural progress of *A Shropshire*

Lad by A. E. Housman [1859-1936] which was published in 1896:

The star-filled seas are smooth to-night
Frome France to England strown;
Black towers above the Portland light
The felon-quarrier stone

On yonder island, not to rise,
Never to stir forth free,
Far from his folk a dead lad lies,
That once was friends with me.

Portland Prison then comprised the buildings at The Grove (SY 700 726) which are now the Young Offenders' Institution. Its convicts were there for hard labour – rising the stone that would enclose four square miles of sea inside the breakwaters of Portland Harbour.

Howard – SDV navigator **Sergeant Richard Howard** [1936-94] of the Special Boat Squadron drowned in Portland Harbour when the top secret mini-submarine pulled him underwater [April 1994].

I

HMS *Illustrious* **tragedy** – 29 ratings, attempted to return to the aircraft-carrier after a day in Weymouth, were drowned in Portland Harbour when their motor-pinnace was swamped in heavy seas [17 October 1948]. There were 22 survivors, which needed some explaining as the vessel was only permitted to carry a total of forty men. Midshipman R. A. Clough, who was among the drowned, was blamed by the subsequent enquiry for this overloading, and failing to turn back on hitting rough water.

Isle of Slingers – Thomas Hardy's name, in his novel *The Well-Beloved* [1892] for the Isle of Portland. It was inspired by the fact that Chesil Beach pebbles, used by prehistoric man as slingstones, had been unearthed from Iron Age hill-forts such as Maiden Castle, near Dorchester.

J

Jacob's Well – see entry for **Hiram Otter**.

Jones – architect **Inigo Jones** [1573-1652] pioneered the use of Portland limestone as the nation's capital building stone, with his rebuilding of the Banqueting Hall in Whitehall [1619-22]. It would be the building in which Charles I was beheaded [1649].

K

Keeve's – see entry for **Cave Hole**.

Kimberlin – Portland word for a mainlander, used as an epithet of disapproval towards outsiders.

King's Pier – most of the stone for St Paul's Cathedral [1675-1716] came from the quarries of East Weares and was shipped from Portland's eastern seaboard (SY 702 735).

Kroger – Soviet agents **Peter Kroger** [1910-95] and wife **Helen** [died 1992] were at the heart of the Portland spy ring. They had two radio transmitters in their bungalow at Ruislip, Middlesex.

Peter Kroger had been born Morris Cohen in the Bronx, New York, fought as Israel Altman against Franco in the Spanish Civil War, and married his abrasive wife, real name Lona, in 1941. They worked for English-born Soviet master-spy Colonel Rudolph Ivanovitch Abel and became principal founders of the Rosenberg spy ring which obtained American's atomic secrets and enabled the Soviet Union to explode its own atom bomb [1948].

They fled to Paris, obtaining Canadian passports which enabled them to proceed to London [1950] where Morris Cohen established a new and semi-respectable identity as an antiquarian bookseller, from 190 The Strand, titillating the Americana with a sideline into pornography.

Even after the breaking of the Portland spy ring, following inquiries by MI5 investigator William "Jim" Skardon, and the finding of their code-pads and microdot reader, neither MI5 or Special Branch had any idea of the Krogers' real identity. That came only after the chance recognition of Peter Kroger as Morris Cohen after an American journalist spotted a news photograph.

The Krogers were each sentenced to 20 years but would be released in exchange for small-fry Gerald Brooke to the fury of MI5 [1969]. They departed for Moscow. It was left to a future owner of the Ruislip bungalow to find their second radio transmitter, which was unearthed in the garden [1977].

L

HMS *Landrail* – redundant cruiser which sank in Lyme Bay after being used for target practice by the Channel Fleet from Portland Harbour [1906]. She had been stripped and filled with dust, ashes, empty barrels, and other semi-inert material, in order to absorb impacts without being set on fire. The battleships HMS *Albemarle*, *Exmouth*, *Prince George*, and *Triumph* closed to within 3,000 yards of her, after beginning from 7,000 yards, as she was being held on a long line from a destroyer.

Lano's Bridge – though vandalised, this is the best preserved of what were once a series of expertly constructed arches and drystone walls that carried sections of the Merchants' Railway through the Tout Quarries, Portland. The lines operated at two levels with the lower rails taking worked stone outwards, and the upper ones generally going at ninety degrees to the main system and being used for push-and-tip wagons that dumped quarry waste over the West cliff. Splendid little bridges were constructed where one part of the network crossed another.

Lawnsheds – the open mediaeval strip-fields of Portland, particularly those on the cliff-side immediately north of the Admiralty Underwater Weapons Establishment, Southwell (SY 680 703). They survive on the island not just because of its insular customs but due to the fact that shared land-tenure has had more than agricultural possibilities given the potential for future quarrying.

LCT *A2454* – tank landing craft, washed on to the Chesil Beach at Wyke Regis in mountainous seas [13 October 1944]. The state of the sea prevented the Weymouth lifeboat and a Portland dockyard tug from coming round Portland Bill to its aid.

Ten of the craft's British crew were drowned, despite heroic efforts by the Fortuneswell Lifesaving Company who had run along the pebble bank from Portland and fired a rocket-line into the striken vessel.

Two of the rescuers – Coastguard Treadwell and Captain Pennington Legh – were also swept to their deaths. In all, four of the sailors were saved; two of those by the lifesavers who were drowned.

The four surviving rescuers were awarded Lloyd's silver medal for lifesaving but one, V. F. Stephens of Wyke Regis, died in a car crash before he could receive it at the reception in Weymouth Guildhall. Cyril Brown of Portland, who struggled through the waves to free a fouled line to the landing craft and then had to be hauled ashore himself and taken to hospital, was awarded the Stanhope Medal for the bravest deed of 1944.

Lee – the man they couldn't hang, **John (Babbacombe) Lee** [born 1862] had the noose around his neck three times in Exeter Gaol [23 February 1885] but on each occasion the lever was pulled, the trapdoor jammed. Sentence was then postponed and afterward commuted to life imprisonment.

Lee had been convicted of the murder of Mrs Keyse, a former lady-in-waiting to Queen Victoria. Her throat had been cut and skull fractured in a frenzied attack, after which the killer set fire to her home, at Babbacombe near Torquay [16 November 1884].

Her footman, John Lee, had a criminal record for theft and was an obvious suspect though he proclaimed his innocence throughout and no direct evidence would be produced at his trial. He would be sentenced to death but upon the failure of the execution an assortment of omens and dreams were said to have predicted the outcome. A flock of white doves circling the prison yard were taken to be a sign of his innocence.

In tests the trap-door to the gallows functioned perfectly but it failed each time that Lee stood on it. This was despite, at the third attempt, a warden jumping on and off it as the hangman tried to free the pulleys.

Then, after the longest 45 minutes of his life, Lee was led back to his cell. On being reprieved he was taken to Portland Prison, then in

John Lee: the man they couldn't hang.

the present Youth Offenders' Institution buildings at The Grove, to serve his life sentence; to be kept inside for 22 years.

His release was as a living legend, with media attention, songs, comic strips and even an early cinema film. The truth, which was that the evidence upon which he had been convicted was circumstantial, became twisted into ever more far-fetched fictions. These had either the dead woman's solicitor being blamed for the murder, or King Edward VII, who as the Prince of Wales had been a frequent visitor to the house in Babbacombe. Lee made up for some of his lost years by marrying a nurse.

Lerret – Portland's own form of rowing boat, pointed at both ends for quick changes of direction into the fierce breakers off the Chesil Beach.

Lighthouses – Sir John Clayton was awarded a patent to erect a lighthouse on the Bill of Portland, [1699] and to show two lights from this tower.

He failed to proceed with this consent, and the first lighthouses, a pair, would be built in 1716. Trinity House had obtained a patent [May 1716] and granted a lease to William Barrett and Francis Browne for £100.

Charles Langridge stoked the coals to illuminate their glazed lanterns for the first time [29 September 1716].

Barrett and Brown were to build and maintain "one or more convenient lighthouses with good and visible lights to be kept continually there in the night season, so as ships might the better come to their ports without peril". The Customs Office, London, was instructed to collect dues from all ships passing the light, at a rate of a halfpenny per ton levied on English ships, and a penny a ton from foreign vessels.

The Lower Light (SY 681 690) was reconstructed in 1789 and was 63 feet high. Both it and the Higher or Upper Light (SY 677 693) were demolished and rebuilt in 1869. The Shambles sandbanks, offshore, had been marked by a lightship [1 May 1859].

The current lighthouse (SY 678 684) described in the entries for Portland Bill, was constructed in 1903-05. Both the redundant lighthouses – the old Higher or Upper Lighthouse and Lower Lighthouse – survive. At the other side of the island, at the eastern end of the North-Eastern Breakwater (SY 704 763), another new lighthouse came into use [14 March 1905].

Limekiln Cave – massive sea cave on Portland's east coast, between Southwell and Portland Bill (SY 689 696). Forty feet inland is a sizable blow-hole, capped with an iron grill.

Lloyd's Cottage – the former Lloyd's Signal Station in an Edwardian bungalow on the rise above Portland Bill, next to a compound which still bristles with masts (SY 678 691).

Lobb – bomb disposal expert **Captain Michael Lobb** [born 1968] spent 31 hours without sleep to defuse an unexploded wartime bomb in a controlled explosion that immobilised its detonator [3 April 1995]. He was feted as a local hero by 4,000 residents as they returned to their homes.

Throughout his ordeal, Captain Lobb of the Royal Engineers, had a letter in his breast pocket from local schoolgirl Laura Gates: "I think you and your Army are very brave and I would like to thank you for your help."

Captain Lobb, by now enjoying champagne and congratulations from returning islanders, told reporters: "The low point of the operation was when I spent six and a half hours drilling a hole into the outer casing of the bomb. It took much longer than I had expected but once it was finished I knew I was on the home run."

Nine so-called "Refuseniks" risked arrest and then injury by insisting on remaining in their homes. They were eventually allowed to stay, after signing disclaimers, while police cordoned off the island to prevent looting.

"That bit was quite easy," an officer said. "The barriers are already there, but we normally use them to try and prevent prisoners leaving rather than mainlanders arriving."

The Longstone – see entry for **Portland megaliths**.

Lonsdale – Soviet masterspy **Gordon Lonsdale**, the operational cover-name of the KGB's Colonel Conon Trimofovich Molody, was the ring leader of the Portland spy cell which infiltrated the top secret Admiralty Underwater Weapons Establishment at Southwell, Portland. He was sentenced to 25 years imprisonment at the Old Bailey [1961] but would be swapped in Berlin for British spy Greville Wynne [1964].

Lovell-Gregg – heroic New Zealander **Squadron Leader Terence Lovell-Gregg** [1913-40] led the Hurricanes of 87 Squadron into impossible odds, over the sea off Portland, at the height of the Battle of Britain. There was no hesitation or deviation. "Come on chaps, let's surround them!" were his last words. "Shovel" and his men were outnumbered by the Luftwaffe fifteen-to-one as they hurtled into action, from 18,000 feet, at 18.00 hours on 15 August 1940.

His fighter was shot to pieces but he might just have survived if the

Mackerel catch: drawn up on the Chesil Beach.

burning aeroplane had not clipped an oak in the wood beside Abbotsbury Swannery. He fell to his death and is buried in the RAF plot at Warmwell churchyard.

L24 – on 10 January 1924, HM Submarine *L24* was rammed by the battle-cruiser HMS *Resolution* in Lyme Bay, to the west of Portland Bill, and sank with all 43 officers and men.

LST507 and *LST531* – tank landing ships sunk by German E-boats west of Blacknor Fort, Portland, whilst en route to the big Exercise Tiger practice landings at Slapton Sands, Devon [27-28 April 1944]. *LST289* was damaged by a torpedo. Five other landing ships, sailing in convoy from the Solent, escaped as the German vessels withdrew with the arrival on the scene of HMS *Azalra* and HMS *Saladin*.

A total of 441 United States soldiers, mainly engineers, were killed or drowned and 197 seamen also lost their lives.

Lucky stones – Portlanders were reluctant to put to sea without a pebble with a natural hole, attached by twine to the stem-post. The superstition was general along the Chesil Beach, westwards to Abbotsbury and Burton Bradstock.

Lynx – Royal Navy anti-submarine helicopter [from 1978]

which gradually replaced the Wasp and took over completely at Royal Naval Air Station Portland when these were finally decommissioned [1988].

M

Maastricht – Dutch merchant vessel, sailing in convoy FN 366, sunk by German E-boats east of Portland Bill [23 December 1940].

Mackerel – news of the sighting of an offshore shoal, approaching Chiswell from Lyme Bay, would bring out fishermen in their lerret rowing-boats. Working in tandem these would round-up shoals of countless thousands of fish with seine nets, and then draw them inshore to land on the pebbles of Chesil Beach.

Madeleine Tristan – a French grain-carrying three-mast schooner, battered on to the shingle of Chesil Cove [20 September 1930].

The sea washed her high on to the beach and she was to be years in breaking up.

Maidenwell – the upper end of Chiswell Square, where the road inland turns towards Fortuneswell and becomes the High Street (SY 684 734). Mallams and King Street rise to the north-west and Green Close lay to the south, towards Alleluia Bay.

Both Mallams and King Street have extensive terraces of 18th and 19th century dates. The Palladian once-ruined Old House crowns the central position between the southern end of these streets.

Mantle – fatally wounded pom-pom gunner **Jack Mantle** [1917-40] continued firing as "Stuka" dive-bombers sank the anti-aircraft auxiliary HMS *Foylebank* in Portland Harbour. His legs had been shattered as bombs tore the ship apart. Of her 179 crew, 59 were killed and 60 injured in the attack, which came at the onset of the Battle of Britain [4 July 1940]. Leading Seaman Mantle, from Southampton, had gone to school at Affpuddle. He was buried in Portland Naval Cemetery, on the Verne Common hillside overlooking the dockyard and harbour and would be gazetted for the Victoria Cross – the first to be won for the Royal Navy inside British territorial waters.

Marriage runaways – traditionally, a Portland church wedding was only for the "kimberlins" – mainlanders, they are – as native islanders were considered married after they had gone through a bizarre communal courting ritual of jumping over a long-handled quarrying shovel.

Substantiation of this has been claimed from a study of the marriage registers for Portland. These reach back to 1591 but for several years there are no entries for people with the three commonest Portland family names – Pearce, Comben, and Stone. Instead, there are many names of non-Portlanders, coming from as far as Yorkshire. They do not seem to have married Portland girls, which is not surprising as the island had a tradition of being a self-sufficient, insular community that rarely absorbed outsiders.

The inference is that these couples were runaway marriages. Portland could only be reached by ferry from Wyke Regis, though that may not have been the main attraction. Legally, by custom rather than any written constitution, Portland functioned almost as a separate state – in a similar way to the Channel Islands today – and mainland Dorset had little control over its affairs.

Masons – see entry for **Portland Masons**.

Massacres – see entries for **Easton Pond Massacre** and the **Slapton Sands Massacre**.

HMS *Matapan* – the new 2,780-ton destroyer *Matapan* went to sea for only six days and was then mothballed at Devonport for the next 22 years [1947-69]. She was then earmarked for special duties, being towed to Portsmouth and reconstructed as the experimental ship on attachment to the Underwater Weapons Establishment at Portland, replacing the 2,240-ton frigate HMS *Verulam*.

These changes cost £2,500,000 and were almost total, involving the strengthening of the hull and removal of her guns and torpedo tubes so that the fo'castle deck could be extended to provide space for scientific laboratories and staff. An extra funnel was added, plus a new bridge and mast, and a bulbous bow would be the housing for Sonar submarine detection equipment.

After undergoing sea trials for three months the vessel was commissioned and sailed for Portland [1972]. Her name commemorates Admiral of the Fleet Sir John Cunningham's victory over the Italian navy at Cape Matapan in 1941.

McKeown – veteran navy flyer **Captain David (Paddy) McKeown** [retired 1977] was the commander of HMS *Osprey*, the Portland shore base. His 35 years flying service for the Royal Navy had taken him up

'Madeleine Tristan': majestic in distress, in Chesil Cove in 1930.

in 52 different types of aircraft, for a total of 4,500 hours airborne, and involved 800 deck landings on sixteen different aircraft carriers. He had survived a mid-air collision in a Corsair over southern India in 1945. He was mentioned in despatches when flying a Sea Fury from HMS *Ocean* in the Korean War, and again in 1956 whilst flying Sea Hawks from HMS *Albion* at Suez.

Mediterranean Scaly Cricket – see entry for (The) **Small Mouth**.

Megaliths – see entry for **Portland Megaliths**.

Meknes – Vichy French liner sunk after being torpedoed by German submarine *U-572* off Portland [24 July 1940]. She was carrying 1,100 neutral French sailors, of whom some 400 were killed.

Merchants' Railway – the narrow gauge stone-carrying railway of the freemen of Portland was named Freeman's Incline, or the Merchants' Railway as it was known in latter years, to differentiate it from the convict-operated Breakwater Railway Incline on the east side of the island.

Freeman's Incline was a steep cable-worked incline operating on the principle that the loaded wagons descending hauled empty ones back to the top. It stretched from Priory Corner to the stone quays at Castletown Pier.

The railway, unlike the majority of those already in existence in the north of England, was a public company authorised by Act of Parliament, incorporated on 10 June 1825 and opened in October 1826. J. H. Lucking says in *Railways of Dorset* that the company, though it has physical assets, is likely to continue in existence indefinitely since an Act of Parliament would be needed to dissolve it.

The incline, which ceased operation in 1940, snakes around the west side of Verne Citadel, Now H. M. Prison, and though trackless there are still two well preserved arms that come up on to the top of the island at the east end of Verne

Merchants' Railway: carried stone down to Castletown, being seen in operation and retirement, as a public footpath (opposite).

Yeates (SY 693 734) and then skirt its northern slope together on a gradual climb to the Prior Corner Commit above the Chesil Beach. An offshoot comes straight on to the island at the Citadel end.

There is a remarkable series of tall neatly-arched Victorian stone bridges and the main incline is now Portland public footpath number 76, with path 77 forking beneath Verne Citadel and path 85 continuing along the course of the railway up the side of Verne Yeates.

Methodist Church – at Easton (SY 691 719), built in early-English style [1906-07].

Missionary shipwreck – Methodist preacher Rev Edward Peard, with 16 others on board, perished when a schooner outward bound from Gravesend for West African was smashed to pieces on the Chesil Beach [29 November 1838].

Molody – top Russian spymaster **Colonel Conon Trimofivch Molody** operated in Britain under the cover-name Gordon Lonsdale and ran an espionage cell inside the Admiralty Underwater Weapons Establishment at Southwell, Portland [1960-61].

HMS **Monarch** – in the failing light on a January afternoon in 1925 the Atlantic Fleet sailed out of Portland to destroy one of its capital ships. She was the 25,000-ton battleship HMS *Monarch*. But unlike most of the vessels that have gone down in target practice before or since there was nothing defective about the *Monarch*. She was only 13 years old.

The *Monarch* had been formally sacrificed under the provisions of the Washington Treaty, an international accord limiting naval armament. Signed in 1922, the treaty was the strategic arms limitation enactment of its day. There was a three year lapse before its provisions became operative. The navy decided that the *Monarch* would be destroyed by her own kind.

The empty ship was hit first with a series of seaplane attacks, which did little, and she then survived a pounding from the 6-inch guns of a line of light cruisers. These hardly dented her armour, the steel of which was a foot thick. Next came the battleships, firing from twelve miles, with each salvo weighing six tons. Eight shells were fired, and some hit but ricocheted to land in the sea miles away. This process lasted all day and the battlecruisers carried on into the night, illuminating their target with great sheets of light stretching across the horizon.

She took it all, and the navy's photographic ship – the aptly named *Snapdragon* – sailed round to record the detail of the damage. The final moments were approaching. The battlecruiser *Repulse* sailed in from her firing position, to within a mile of the *Monarch*. She fired into the crippled hulk, aiming at the waterline, tearing a hole to let the sea into the hull. The *Monarch* listed and gradually sank from view of the searchlights.

Museum – see entry for **Portland Museum**.

Myrtledene – steamship laden with iron-ore, wrecked in Mutton Cove, Portland [25 March 1912]. She had been sailing up-Channel, for Rotterdam, and ended up wedged bow-first in the offshore rocks (SY 678 712).

N

USS *Nautilus* – world's first nuclear submarine [built 1954] visited Portland Dockyard [October 1957], returning in triumph after achieving the first voyage under the North Pole [10 August 1958].

On the earlier visit she was welcomed to Britain by the First Sea Lord, Louis Mountbatten, and Defence Minister Duncan Sandys,

Naval Cemetery: seen from Verne Citadel, guarding Portland Harbour.

who would take the Royal Navy down the nuclear option.

Naval base – created beside and around the stone quays east of Castletown [1857] to service warships sheltering in the man-made Portland Harbour, as it took shape in Victorian times as the biggest in Europe.

Became a main base for the battleships of the Home Fleet and the setting for numerous naval reviews. Jetties provided moorings for destroyers and other escort vessels. Submarines and aircraft-carriers followed as the Great War was followed by the Second World War.

The proximity of the Luftwaffe and E-boats, operating from the Cherbourg peninsula, limited its role in the latter conflict until it became the main-base for the American First Army units tasked to invade Omaha Beach, on D-Day [6 June 1944].

Principal operational and secret research base for anti-submarine warfare throughout the Cold War. Rapprochement and the end of communism would see the departure of its final fleet – sea training for the frigates, and all the Royal Navy's surface ships, would henceforth be carried out from Plymouth.

Closure of Portland naval base took place on the departure of HMS *Argyll*, and the 250 staff of the Sea Training Centre, for Devonport [22 July 1995]. Eleven admirals

attending the ceremony in which the White Ensign was lowered and a 13-gun salute fired. The First Sea Lord, Admiral Sir Jock Slater, sent a signal praising Portland's "outstandingly successful" association with the Royal Navy.

Nelson – pioneer island Methodist **William Nelson** [1711-70] is buried in St George's churchyard.

New Ground – the parking area beside Yeats Road, Portland (SY 691 731) and adjoining sports pitches were cleared of rocks by convicts and levelled in the 1870s to provide the defenders of Verne Citadel with a clear field of fire.

Nicodemus Knob – rough lozenge-shaped rock left standing about 30 feet high by quarrying on the west side of Portland's plateau (SY 699 729). These were the Admiralty Quarries, opened by the Victorians for building the Breakwaters of Portland Harbour. Rather than being intended as a sea-mark, the stone is more likely to have been cut for a boundary "at the east part of the Common or Weir" – Weare being the Portland name for a cliff.

It seems to have taken its name from Nicodemus Knowle, which was in use until Victorian times for the cliff beneath the prison.

Nor – Norwegian steamship washed up and stranded on the

Chesil Beach [18 January 1887]. The crew were brought off safely by rocket apparatus. The vessel later broke her back and was eventually smashed to pieces.

Norval – a Plymouth schooner which had the distinction of being the first vessel to be wrecked by Portland's new Harbour of Refuge [30 January 1861]. She was thrown against the stonework of the Inner Breakwater in a gale. The crew of five were saved.

O

Nicodemus Knob: seamark left by quarrying, on the eastern cliffs.

Oath of the island – "On the word of a Portland man."

O'Donovan Rossa – Irish rebel **Jeremiah O'Donovan Rossa** was among the members of the Fenian Brotherhood held in Portland Prison [1866-69]. His release was brought forward after a letter was smuggled to the press in which he told of horrific conditions on the island, and by election in his absence for the constituency of Tipperary to the Westminster Parliament. He never took his seat. Having won his freedom he led the Irish American pressure for Home Rule and survived an assassination attempt on the streets of New York, being gunned down by a young British widow.

Oil Tanks – Royal Naval fuel depot beside the former railway line and Portland's A354 approach road, on The Mere (SY 680 744). Initially there were two tanks, for innovative oil-burning warships [1901] but the number eventually reached 26.

Fourteen of them are currently in a line that stretches for half a mile beside the main road.

The Old House – at Maidenwell, the lower end of the High Street, Fortuneswell (SY 684 733) looks out across the Chesil Beach. Or rather, its Palladian grey-stone window mullions and impressive 18th century pedimented porch face in that direction – for there is no one to look through them. It is quite the best bit of architecture around and how it came to be abandoned, to fall into roofless ruin, is a complete mystery.

It has been this way for all of living memory and far beyond, though restoration plans have now been approved [1996]. Old men have tales, but they are all different – ranging from the dream home of a young gentleman who was jilted and left Portland, to the home of two brothers who sailed to Australia and abandoned their link with the old country.

Another story, more persuasive, is that the builders were a working class couple who ran out of money. There is the look about it of incompleteness rather than collapse, though it is said to have been the home of Dr Motger.

John Murphy gave me the version he tended to believe, which he had heard from an old Portlander in 1977:

"He tells of the rich old lady who decided to have a house built. Her plans extended further than the years left to her and she died before the final building stage. Relatives showed no inclination to continue with her project, and the building was abandoned. Only the garden was used the giant cellars turned into store rooms. The last owner died just four years ago, leaving no heirs. One day the property will go to the crown."

Not that it is a complete waste. Around it there is a grassy slope, itself a rarity in densely urban Fortuneswell, and inside there are

Old House: remembered as a romantic ruin.

often the cries of children at play. When I made my inspection some years back a young girl came to the door – astride a white pony. But then, as we are told, you can take a white horse anywhere!

Omolphus rufitarus – half-inch long and one of Britain's rarest beetles, believed to feed on pollen of the thrift flower, *Ameria maritima*, but only in limited locations such as the western end of the Chesil Beach, Abbotsbury, where it grows on shingle that adjoins a salt marsh. It has a black thorax, chestnut-red wing cases, and six long legs. Recorded also from the Portland and Weymouth end of the shingle but unknown elsewhere in Britain. There was no record of any specimen being found between 1926 and 1989 when a group of ten coleopterists were delighted to find more than a hundred. Howard Mendel spotted the first, crawling on a thrift flower: "I was overjoyed to see it there. We found it in far greater numbers than ever we dreamed. No one knows its life history. The larvae seem to live in the soil beneath the plant."

HMS **Osprey** – command ship of the First Anti-Submarine Flotilla,

HMS Osprey: Portland air base, with **Sea Hawk** in foreground and **Captain David 'Paddy' McKeown** being towed into retirement, 1977.

commissioned in Portland Harbour to run the Royal Navy's Anti-Submarine School [1 April 1924]. The headquarters was moved on shore [1927] and the name would follow it, being revived after the Second World War to assess the potential of anti-submarine helicopters [1946].

This led to the creation of the Royal Naval Air Station [1959], that perpetuated the name HMS *Osprey* at the height of the Cold War and had its airfield created by land reclamation [1967-70] across The Mere (SY 682 743) which was then provided with new accommodation blocks south-east of it [1986].

Otter – quarryman **Hiram Otter** [circa 1855-1940] became a stalwart of Portland's new Salvation Army Corps [1885] and proceeded to create public footpath number 5 which snakes south from Chesil Cove, beneath West Weares, to the headland at Tar Rocks and Clay Ope beyond it (SY 681 724). He used his "large and sinewy arms, with muscles of strong iron bands" to hand-jack immense pieces of stone out of the way.

Then he proceeded to etch biblical inscriptions and the first lines of some of the Salvationists' powerful hymns. "Alleluia!" he would cry when each of these texts was completed.

Alleluia Bay became the local name for the indented coast between Chesil Cove and Tar Rocks (SY 682 727). Silverwell, on the undercliff west of Priory Corner (SY 682 739), was renamed Jacob's Well.

P

Parsonage House – the home of Portland's rector stood in Wakeham. It was reduced to a ruin in the Civil War [1643], being "demolished and burnt down by the Usurper Oliver Cromwell and hasn't been rebuilded ever since".

Passage boat – the ferry at Small Mouth (SY 668 762), the only access on to the island, from Wyke Regis, until the building there of the Ferrybridge [1839]. The boat was drawn from side to side by hand-holds on a suspended rope.

Patria – Norwegian barque which lost a man overboard in a squall, whilst en route from Frederickstad to Durban with a cargo of timber, and then shed most of her sails as she attempted to turn into Portland Roads [26 October 1903]. She was then driven into West Bay (SY 680 738) as onlookers from Chiswell waded into the waves to pull the remaining crew of eleven to safety.

HMT *Pelton* – Royal Navy armed trawler sunk by German E-boats whilst escorting convoy FN 366 east of Portland Bill [23 December 1940].

Penn – poet, dramatist and very rich, **John Penn** [1760-1834] of Stoke Poges Park, Buckinghamshire, built Pennsylvania Castle, Portland [1800]. He was the grandson of William Penn [1644-1718] who founded the American state of Pennsylvania.

Though unmarried, John Penn founded a "matrimonial society" to improve the domestic life of married persons. His greatest success on the stage was *The Battle of Eddington, or British Liberty*, about King Alfred and the Danes, which was performed at Windsor, the Haymarket, Covent Garden and Sadler's Well.

A handbill of December 1829, displayed in Portland Museum, shows that his life and wealth and privilege was not universally respected as revolution swept Europe. It offers £100 reward for the arrest of the men who wrote a letter demanding £50 from the island's Governor Penn, saying:

Pennsylvania Castle: William Penn's jewellery cabinet, on view in 1921.

"One of us will step into the castle and leave this letter; what we want you will not miss, you have so much, so much more than you ever can want, much more than you deserve, while others have not the necessaries of life."

Pennsylvania Castle – among Penn's trees which are the sycamores of the only wood on the island, at the south end of Wakeham's wide street, was built for John Penn [1760-1834] to the designs of eminent architect James Wyatt [1746-1813] in 1800. It is Gothic mock-fortification with matching embattled parapets to the gateway (SY 695 711).

The double pun in the name was that Penn's grandfather William Penn [1644-1718] had founded Pennsylvania.

As for John Penn of Portland, he was a reasonably prolific writer, poet and dramatist. In 1817 he formed a "matrimonial society" to improve the domestic life of married persons. It became the Outlinian Society, 1818-25. Penn himself was unmarried.

He was something of a playwright, with *The Battle of Eddington or British Liberty* being performed at Windsor, the Haymarket, Covent Garden and Sadler's Wells. He also translated Virgil and wrote his own poems, published on the private press at his other seat, Stoke Poges Park in Buckinghamshire. There is a memorial to him in St George's church, at Reforne on Portland.

Peto seaplane – built by George Parnall and Company at Bristol and housed in a hangar built beside the big Royal Navy submarine *M2* [launched 1919] which was recommissioned as an aircraft-carrier [1927]. She had a 28-feet wing-span that folded to only 8 feet. Experimental flights achieved a maximum speed of 113 miles per hour and endurance times of two hours in the air. What seemed like hopeful progress came to an abrupt halt off Dorset, three miles west of Portland Bill, when the submarine dived with its hangar doors open or faulty, letting in the sea [10.30 hours, 26 January 1932].

She sank to 17 fathoms and the entire crew of 60 submariners – including ten who operated the doors and Peto's pilot – were drowned. The tiny seaplane was later raised but out of respect for the dead it was decided that she should be scrapped, and the project died with her. Salvage attempts to lift the huge submarine were eventually abandoned [8 September 1932] and she was left as a tomb. Divers say the 305-feet hull is still intact, perhaps because it sits on sand, and that the hangar doors remain open.

Pierston – fictional Portland sculptor **Jocelyn Pierston** is the main male character in Thomas Hardy's novel *The Well-Beloved* [1892], which is set on the island.

Portland Bill Lighthouse – took the place of the old Upper and Lower Lighthouses. Work begun in October 1903. Trinity House paid £300 for the site and the circular stone tower was built by contractors Wakeham Brothers of Plymouth. Work finished in 1905.

The same year, on 14 March, another new Portland lighthouse – on the east end of the North-Eastern Breakwater – was also used for the first time.

The earliest lighthouses on Portland Bill, a pair, were erected in 1716 and the lower one was reconstructed in 1789. Both were pulled down and rebuilt in 1869. The first lightship to be anchored off the Bill, beside the Shambles sandbank, was placed there on 1 May 1859.

The lighthouse on the Bill has a 136 feet high white-painted circular stone tower with a red band around its middle. Its night-time white flashes are in fact a group of four lights, giving a beam every twenty seconds. This equals 3,370,000 candles and is visible in clear weather for 18 miles. An additional red light illuminates the water over the Shambles sandbank. The lights are set at 141 feet above the high water mark.

There were three keepers in pre-automatic days (lighthouses originally operated with two but when the boat pulled in at remote stations there were cases where they found only one had survived an argument). Visitors are allowed to climb the 153 steps to see the three tons of lens, floating at the top on a liquid metal base – half a ton of mercury.

Closer to ground level, seaward of the tower, the fog horn is activated as visibility falls to less than two miles and gives a blast of three and a half seconds at half minute intervals.

Portland Bill placename – this has its roots in "The Beel" of early maps, apparently deriving from the beak shape of the projecting headland – as in a bird's bill – has almost entirely eclipsed its other local name. From 1588 onwards, when it had a crucial bonfire in the Armada invasion-warning network, it was known as The Beacon.

Here the beacon chain turned the corner, from the last of the Lyme Bay flares on the great cliff at Thorncombe Beacon, and signalled its warning to St Alban's Head in the Purbeck quarrylands. From there, via Beacon Hill at Lytchett Minster and St Catherine's Hill above Christchurch, the pivotal point in the network was on the Isle of Wight. There the watchers could

Portland Bill: the Lighthouse.

Portland Bill: sunset over Lyme Bay.

pass the alert directly inland, to Southampton, Winchester and London, as well as to the Sussex coast.

Portland Bird Observatory – in the island's former Lower Lighthouse. This was erected in 1716, reconstructed in 1789, and demolished and rebuilt in its present form in 1869 (SY 680 688).

Turned into a bird observatory in 1961, it is one place in southern England where melodious and icterine warblers are dependable annual appearances for ornithologists. Some two thousand birds make their landfall into waiting mist-nets.

Warblers are a speciality, including the aquatic warbler, Bonelli's warblers, sub-Alpine warblers and yellow-browed warblers. Occasionally there is the excitement of American visitors that are freak windfalls from the jet stream.

Portland Castle – Dorset's only intact mediaeval castle is a low, solid stone fortress with walls of massive thickness intended to withstand the new age of gunpowder (SY 684 743). Built in 1520 by Henry VIII it was part of a master plan to protect the Channel coast from surprise attack and is at the west of a long string of forts. Hurst Castle in Hampshire, at the mouth of the Solent, is the strongest and these new-style

castles have played a part in coastal defence during every European war since the 16th century – including the last.

In the Civil War it was one of the first places garrisoned for Parliament but it changed hands and was later one of the last pockets of royalist resistance in the west. It held ordnance and prisoners and was the intact veteran of several sieges. Parliamentary troops attacked it early in the war [1642] and returned several times, though they did not receive its surrender until the end of the war [4 April 1646].

That was with dignity, negotiated by Captain William Batten, Vice-Admiral and Commission-in-Chief of the King Charles's navy, and Colonel Thomas Sidney Gollop, Governor of the Castle and Isle of Portland. They and their officers and soldiers were free to "march away with all their horses, not surmounting the number fifteen, full arms, match alight, bullet in mouth, colours displayed, drums beating, and bag and baggage to Oxford".

Portland Castle was the residence of the Governor of Portland and was strategically placed on the water's edge beside the former Mere at the isthmus of pebbles joining the island to the mainland. It commanded Weymouth Road, the anchorage now enclosed by the breakwaters of Portland Harbour.

Portland Castle:
Henry VIII's coastal fortress remains intact,
beside what is now Portland Harbour.

Sandsfoot Castle, its partner on the other side, has lost its gun-platform over the cliff.

Portland Castle, which is next to the Royal Naval helicopter base that now covers the Mere, is opened to the public by English Heritage.

Portland cement – has nothing to do with Portland, apart from being the man-made substitute for its stone, though the coincidence of the name has led to unlikely statements in print, such as by G. E. Mingay in *Rural Life in Victorian England*: "Cement works appeared around Portland Bill ..." [1977]. The patent for Portland cement was applied for by Leeds bricklayer Joseph Aspdin in 1824.

He mixed chalk with clay and heated the mixture to produce a powder which, when mixed with sand, was found to be impervious. It was reckoned to be as durable as that used by the Romans, though it would seem a little premature to make that sort of claim.

Roman cement has a decayed spongy look but is in fact rock-hard. Its magic ingredient, attributed in Northern folklore to human blood, is in fact calcium silicate hydrate.

Which has even less to do with Portland!

Portland convict poem – the realities of a Portland convict's life interrupt the rural progress of *A*

Shropshire Lad by A. E. Housman [1859-1936] which was published in 1896.

The star-filled seas are smooth to-night
From France to England strown:
Black towers above the Portland light
The felon-quarrier stone

On yonder island, not to rise,
Never to stir forth free,
Far from his folk a dead lad lies,
That once was friends with me

Portland Prison then comprised the buildings at The Grove (SY 700 726) which are now the Borstal. Its convicts were there for hard labour – raising the stone that would enclose four square miles of sea inside the breakwaters of Portland Harbour.

Portland Dough-cake – in 1969 I published an appeal for someone to provide me with its secret recipe. From Portland I received cries of incredulity, such as this from Mrs Lillie Moore of Wakeham: "Do you seriously think any self-respecting Portlander would give you the recipe?"

One Portlander did, however, via Mrs Mary E. Bradley of Durweston: "I returned yesterday from Odstock Hospital. Near me was a lady from Portland and friends brought her sister. As I had no visitors that afternoon they were pleased to leave the two sisters together and talk to me. We talked 'Portland' and then I suddenly remembered your request for Portland dough cake. The lady had made 30 lbs at Christmas and distributed it amongst friends and neighbours. This is the recipe the Tomkins checked and double-checked between them and gave me:

2 lbs dough (as for bread)
1¹/₂ lbs currants
1 lb lard (this is the usual amount
but if a very rich mixture is
desired add ¹/₄ lb butter)
¹/₄ lb brown sugar
¹/₄ lb mixed peel
1 teaspoon of nutmeg

"The least possible plain flour needed on your hands to knead the mixture. Press out, naturally, and cook. We didn't go into oven temperatures as it was taken for granted that cooks would know."

After the Portland sisters had returned to the island and its traditional diet they wrote to Mrs Bradley and divulged another of the secret tastes of Portland, its rice-cake:

"We thought you might like a recipe for a rice-cake. It is a lovely cake. I do cook mine for ³/₄ hour in a gas oven at a high regulo of number four then down to number two, just like a rich fruit cake (and also slow cooking for Portland dough-cake). My friend suggests

that we use ³/₄ lard and ¹/₄ butter, as some people do not like it too rich.

10 ozs s.r. flour
6 ozs lard
4 ozs margarine
4 ozs brown sugar
1 lb currants
4 ozs ground rice
2 eggs
1 teaspoonful of vinegar
1¹/₂ teaspoonful nutmeg
and spice
1¹/₂ teaspoonful bicarbonate
2 ozs peel
1¹/₂ cup of milk

"This should then be cooked slowly for 2¹/₂ to 3 hours at gas regulo two."

Portland Harbour – "THESE ARE IMPERIAL WORKS AND WORTHY KINGS," records a great block of stone at the Castletown end of Portland Breakwater (SY 697 743) though access has been only available on Royal Navy open days. "From this spot on the 25th of July 1849 His Royal Highness Prince Albert, consort of Queen Victoria, sunk the first stone of the breakwater. Upon the same spot, Albert Edward, Prince of Wales, on the 10th of August 1872 laid this last stone and declared the work complete." It was not quite, Portland as an extensive second stage of breakwater building would follow [1894-1903].

Portland Harbour: Fort Head and the Outer Breakwater, looking towards the island from above the East Ship Channel.

A Harbour of Refuge had been provided for the Home Fleet with four square miles of deep water being enclosed behind massive walls of stone. It is bigger than anything created in the colonies and is indeed one of the peaks of British engineering achievement. It is the largest man-made harbour in the world.

Portland already gave natural protection from prevailing south-westerly gales and had itself the rock that would be hewn by convicts – including a healthy and hefty band of Irish republicans – to create a barrier against easterly storms. The rock came less than a mile down the Admiralty Incline from the quarries around The Grove where their prison is a now a Borstal. Much of the stone for the first arm of the breakwater came from the great ditch along the south side of Verne Citadel. Most of this was removed as boulders of up to 6 tons apiece. In all 5,750,000 tons of stone went into the first two arms of the breakwater. The magnitude of the effort was such that it was spread over three decades but that is not to say its pace was slow. The

Portland Harbour: Fort Head defending the East Ship Channel.

Portland Harbour: the North Eastern Breakwater and 'A' Head and Lighthouse, seen from above the East Ship Channel.

record for a week's work was 25,000 tons of stone being dumped into the sea.

The railway lines stretched out with the arms of the breakwater into the sea and ahead of the completed section went a cage of timber scaffolding from which the trucks could dump their loads vertically into the water.

The method had been devised by the engineer James Meadows Rendel [1799-1856] for the deep-water Millbay Pier at Plymouth. The speed with which he could block off the force of the waves was unprecedented. On his death, the project was taken over by John Cooke [1816-92]. Were we a nation that praises famous engineers we would talk of Rendel and Cooke in the same breath as Telford and Smeaton.

Instead, whilst for minor literati there is lasting attention, for the author of an immense work of world-beating size, there is anonymity and silence. Many Dorset guides that go into raptures about such unfunctional things as churches do not even mention the biggest harbour man has yet built on earth, nor the fact that it came in time to play a part in reducing to acceptable proportions the rate of shipwreck casualties that used to bloody our coast.

Portland Harbour is the largest man-made structure in Dorset, and arguably its most important, will last till the end of the world. That it owed so much to slave labour is in the best traditions of architectural achievements across the ancient world.

Victorian notoriety came to Portland with the establishment on the island of Britain's largest penal institution. The choice of Portland for its location was no accident. It was in every way a sensible, hard-headed decision. The navy needed a deep-water harbour of refuge in the mid-west section of the English Channel between Plymouth and Portsmouth.

Often more than a hundred ships would be forced to take cover in Weymouth Bay from the fierce storms raging in the Channel. However choppy it could become in the Portland Roads anchorage the sea here was in no way as deadly as Lyme Bay. There the arm of the Chesil Beach linking Portland with the mainland was nicknamed Deadman's Bay. Ships coming up the Channel, driven by south-westerly winds, had no escape if they failed to round Portland Bill and were trapped in the waters to the west of the island: "In a south-west gale, tremendous seas are to be seen in this fatal bay. Fatal, because a heavy sea running straight in from the Atlantic drives before it, without chance of escape, vessels into this bay. Once vessels are trapped in this way, they are quickly driven upon the beach, and dashed to pieces by the force of the breakers, before assistance can be procured."

Portland was one of the worst black-spots in what had become a major national problem. In the era of sailing ships, the quantity of sinkings made any hope of solutions seem impossible, in the same way that road accidents are accepted today as an inevitable adjunct to our way of life. The loss of valuable shipping and cargo amounted to 4,000 vessels in one year alone. The toll in lives was also considerable and ran at nearly a thousand a year – though this figure is less horrific if you realise that our society stands the loss of 7,000 people in car crashes each year.

Building a breakwater from Portland to create a harbour of refuge had been put forward as a serious suggestion in 1794 but it took many years before the idea was adopted by the Admiralty.

Their interest was given impetus by the French who were set to turn Cherbourg into a great naval fortress. Its breakwaters could shelter the whole of the French navy and its Grand Napoleon Docks would be completed in 1858. It was in response to this massive undertaking in progress across the water that the Portland project was pushed forward with imperial vigour. A Royal Commission in 1843 looked into the success of a breakwater at Plymouth and considered one for Portland was

Portland Harbour: yacht and P297, heading seaward through the North Ship Channel.

Portland Harbour: 'These are Imperial Works and Worthy Kings' states the commemorative stone, laid by the Prince of Wales in 1872.

also feasible, particularly as all the material needed for its construction could be dug from the island itself.

The report costed the project at £500,000, which in retrospect sounds modest. The brainwave came when someone thought about the possibilities of prison labour. A whole prison complex could be built on Portland for the specific purpose of providing cheap labour. The prisoners could be bribed with the prospect of remission in their sentences, and an earlier release on a "ticket of leave".

The country's prison accommodation was anyway overcrowded and needed new outlets. Penal transportation was being resisted as the colonies began to assert their own rights, and crime figures were escalating as a result of the famine and economic depression of the "Hungry Forties". The Home Secretary, Sir George Grey, complained that the Irish regarded a transportation sentence as "a reward rather than a punishment".

In theory, the system demanded that men sentenced to be transported had to serve the "penal" part of their sentence in a British prison before being shipped overseas. The colonies were also flexing political muscle and insisting that they would only accept convicts who had been given a trade.

Grey believed totally in the principles of solitary confinement, religious and education instruction, hard labour and then exile. The inducement was a fair rate of pay on Portland; part was banked on their behalf so that they arrived in the colonies with the work-ethic and some independent means. Perhaps the system was not that harsh, for as Sir Charles Fitz Roy remarked, there "are a few English criminals" who would not delight in receiving "a free passage to the gold-fields via Hobart town". The Times argued that transportation was "a frightful inducement to the commission of crime."

Even with the expulsion of criminals by transportation, and a new prison on Portland, the country's penal establishments – pre-eminently Pentonville – were still hopelessly inadequate and 2,000 men lay in hulks. Officially no more than 10,900 could be accommodated, and then only by distorting the figures and including Gibraltar and Bermuda as British prisons. As the colonies refused to receive more convicts Britain

Portland Harbour: warship pens off the Coaling Pier.

embarked on a hasty prison building programme to increase the accommodation to 16,000.

In the 1840s, as it became clear that Portland would be grasped by the joint tentacles of the Admiralty and Home Office, the island population started to protest. Petitions were drawn up objecting to the prison. The government decided to avoid confrontation, and paid what everyone thought was a generous settlement.

A total of £20,000 was given in 1847 in compensation for the islanders' loss of rights across the extensive areas of common land at Verne and the Weares cliffs. The Portlanders' enthusiasm was muted when the Enclosure Commissioner, who had powers over the allocation of such moneys, insisted that only £10,000 could go to individuals and the rest had to be spent on community projects. Of this, they decided £4,000 would pay off the toll debts on the Ferry Bridge.

In this way the people of Portland lost a fifth of their windfall – in settling tolls which would have been paid by the government in any case. Such was the quantity of men and materials introduced into Portland by the prison, breakwater and harbour construction industries that most of the toll fees would have been charged to the government. Not until July 1851, after Parliament had passed a special act enabling the money to be spent without the islanders' consent, did Portland finally cease objecting and accept the iniquitous settlement imposed for the "public good". The other money went towards improving schools, the Portland Dispensary, and on a more reliable supply of fresh water. These too were benefits which were inevitable given the capital investment and influx of people taking place. The island was having to pay for its own colonisation.

Events took place so fast that the prison was already built and occupied before the money dispute had even started. On 21 November 1848 the first convicts arrived on the island. They came by boat from Portsmouth, on the *Driver* and were landed at Castletown. Weymouth police provided the escort, supported by coastguards Pepperell, Cleall, Ball and Fisher. The men were marched up Verne Hill, across King Barrow and then to the newly finished prison at The Grove.

The extent to which the breakwater was going to be a government prestige project can be gauged from the calibre of the royal group that came to officiate over its opening. One Portlander who, as a child, witnessed Prince Albert's ceremonial stone dropping on 25 July 1849 remembered his school having a holiday for the occasion, and recorded his memories in the 1920s: "There was a large elevated platform full of grandees, and of course no place for me, but I wanted to see the so-called 'laying' and so, eluding official eyes, I got under the platform, which was many feet above my head, and sat on the rocks quite alone.

"When the stone was released it fell through the platform aperture, and in my full view – only a few yards off – plunged into the sea, giving me a parting douche from its splash as it disappeared beneath the water. I consider I had the most perfect view of any present of the sinking of the foundation stone.

"The stone, with its inscription and enclosed collection of current coins and newspapers, was quickly buried under several loads of rough rocks. After this boyish connection with the first stone of the work it was somewhat remarkable that it should have fallen to me to supply the block out of which was shaped the last stone of the structure, the memorial stone, which was laid by King Edward (then Prince of Wales) in August 1872, recording the completion of the undertaking and concluding with the line: 'These are Imperials Works and Worthy Kings.' Prince Albert was always greatly interested in the progress of the breakwater works and often came from Osborne in the royal yacht to inspect them."

The major quarrying area for stone to build the breakwater lay to the north-west of the prison, between The Grove and Verne Hill at the top of East Weares. But before any stone could be removed a route to the bottom had to be cut into the precipitous cliffs. A cable-operated incline railway was already functioning on the north face of the island, to Castletown, and the Admiralty decided on something similar for the eastern cliffs. Navvies (known on Portland as "free-men" to distinguish them from the convict forced labour) constructed an incline from Alma Terrace at The Grove to the starting point for the first arm of the Breakwater, at a point known as Portland Nore.

The slope they built was nearly a mile long and divided into three separate inclines. At the top of each of these was a revolving drum, with steel cables, and these controlled the descent of the trucks. The loaded wagons descending hauled the empty ones back. Two sets of rails were used, one for the loaded trucks and the other for the empties. There was a third set of rails at the beginning when the incline was being constructed. The central incline was not as steep as the upper and lower slopes, the difference being one-in-ten to one-in-fifteen.

Powerful screw-brakes were needed to regulate the descent of trucks of stone. Perhaps the most remarkable fact about this railway was that the ropes of galvanised steel were continuous and had a length of more than two miles. They were tested to a 40-ton breaking strain. All loads passed over a weighbridge at the top and weights were recorded automatically. Visitors were allowed to use the incline when the prisoners were not at work.

The method of bringing the stone down to the sea was almost as ingenious as the engineering techniques that were needed to build the breakwater itself. As the breakwater was built out into the bay, it had to incorporate a wooden platform to carry the railway line, which would be continually extended so that the wagons tipped directly into the sea. The trucks were designed with a trap-door bottom so that they could jettison their load over the chosen point.

This platform looked like a viaduct and needed all the expertise and technology that was then available. It had to stand in eleven fathoms of water, and still rise a reasonable height above sea level. In most places it was running 90 feet above the bottom of the bay.

To hold this sort of structure in the changeable waters of the English Channel called for great logs and a screw-driving capstan. Each log was immersed in a specially constructed vat, a 100 feet long, in which it was saturated under pressure with creosote. Air was pumped out from the chamber and the log itself, which was then bathed in the creosote at a pressure

Portland Harbour: section of wartime Mulberry Harbour, off Portland Castle beach.

of 100 lb per square inch, and left to soak for a couple of days. Finally the logs were bolted into piles and given a Mitchell-type screw head at the bottom end. This is a flat screw of only one-and-a-half thread turns. At the top a cap was fixed to the pole, serrated to grip ropes, and then lowered into position and revolved until it was deep in the clay below the seabed.

When the skeleton of the breakwater "viaduct" was finished, a stage at a time, the railway was extended along the top and the trucks dropped their stone. As each section of the breakwater was completed the timber framework became concealed by the thousands of tons of rock and it remains encased to this day. The work of pile driving, which can be taken for granted once the job is finished, was the crucial part of the whole operation. The men who carried it out were under continuous strain and tension. Historian T. P. Hattersley has pointed out that "even with strong cross-bracing, a storm or violent wave could uproot the structure as if it were made of matchsticks, destroying the works of months in as many minutes".

The first two arms of the breakwater consumed 5,750,000 tons of Portland stone, sometimes at the rate of between 2,000 and 3,000 tons a day. Much of it was in the form of large blocks weighing four to six tons. Pieces of infill were graded from two hundredweight down to pieces of under six inches. Grading was essential to ensure even compaction. The stone was dumped and allowed to settle, and then gouged out to the level of the lowest tides, and reinforced with walls of squared granite blocks. The convicts quarried and prepared the stone. The island's prison population grew to 1,600 of whom seven hundred worked in the quarries and four hundred as masons. Officially the prison, parts of which still had timber walls, was a temporary work camp. Other camps accommodated the "free workmen" – navvies and artisans – who carried out most of the labouring work on the breakwater itself.

The agonies of work on Portland became legendary, and the occasional newsworthy incidents included the execution at Dorchester on 14 August 1869 of a convict named Hatheridge who had killed a prison warder. A mutiny took place at the prison on 12 September 1858 when large numbers of prisoners escaped and were rounded up on Verne Hill.

The first arm of Portland Breakwater ran for 1,800 feet and was completed in 1868. Then came a 400-foot gap – the southern entrance – followed by the second arm which ran for 7,500 feet and was completed in 1872. These two arms totalled a mile and three-quarters and gave shelter to an area calculated at about two square miles.

Again, as recognition for its national significance, the work attracted a royal visitor. The Prince of Wales (later King Edward VII) came to lay the requisite stone: "From this spot on the 25th of July 1849 His Royal Highness Prince Albert, Consort of Queen Victoria, sunk the first stone of this Breakwater.

"Upon the same spot Albert Edward, Prince of Wales, on the 18th of August 1872 laid this last stone.

"These are Imperial Works and Worthy Kings."

Their cost had escalated to a million pounds, and would go higher when the breakwaters were given two forts as finishing touches. One, at the outer end of the first section, was built in granite with a wooden drawbridge separating it from the breakwater. Guarding this moat were eight 64 lb guns. Once fired along the sea-walls, towards the island, and the others guarded the circumference. Yet this was only a light pill-box compared with the massive circular fort that was placed at the end of the second section, more than a mile out into the sea.

Here was built the most futuristic in appearance of all the Victorian South Coast forts. It looks like a flying saucer, having a wide sloping surround with a dome-shaped middle. In profile it is lower and more streamlined than the forts of Spithead which are the closest comparisons. As for size, it is enormous – far larger than you would think from mainland glimpses. The walls at the sides are laminated iron sheets infilled with concrete more than 12 feet across and the dome at the top was originally open, and then closed with sheets of iron mounted upon girders. It had seven 12.5 inch rifled muzzle loading cannon. Some of these, perhaps all, lie in the water of the south-east corner where they were dumped when breach-loading six-inch guns superseded them. Each cannon weighs 38 tons; its carriage and platform weighed a further 12 tons.

A structure this size had its problems. Settlement difficulties in 1868 required patching up on an enormous scale:

"The force of the sea is very great here and some hundreds of tons of stone are often sent across the harbour in a day to repair the breaches made by the sea in the foundations of the outer fort."

Fort Head, this "outer fort" of Portland Breakwater, was conceived as one of a chain of defences. To the north-west, 3,400 yards away across Portland Bay, was the Nothe Fort at Weymouth. Overlooking the new harbour from the heights at

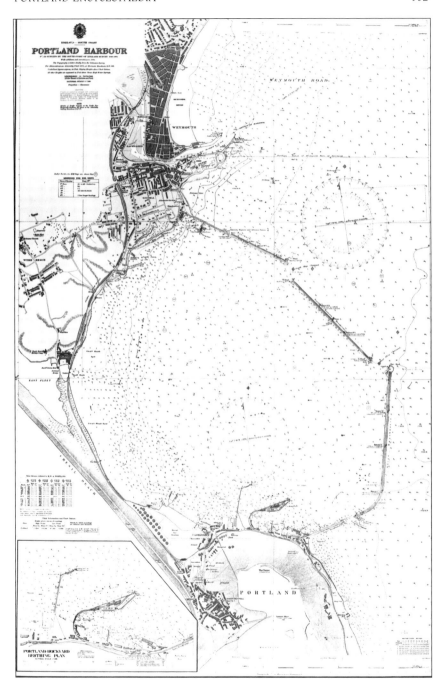

Portland Harbour: its Victorian breakwaters enclose four square miles of deep water.

the top of Portland was the fortress of Verne Citadel and coastal gun batteries at East Weare. The fire-power of the latter should have totalled seven 10-inch and thirteen 9-inch guns but this was never achieved because one battery could not be built, due to subsidence.

The project outlasted all its participants. James Meadows Rendel, designer of the breakwater, died in 1856. John Cooke, a Cornish engineer, took over and earned a knighthood for his work and a commission from the colonial government of South Africa to build a similar "Harbour of Refuge" in Table Bay. Cooke established a science of dock and harbour engineering as an exportable field for British expertise.

There was, however, a long lapse at Portland. Work on the breakwaters had stopped in 1872 but 20 years later, when Cooke died, the Portland project was still not completed but merely suspended.

Victorian morality appears overriding, but when it came to a choice between religion and armaments the latter had priority. Only in 1872, when the initial breakwater and fortification scheme was completed, was labour directed into building a church at The Grove for the prison officers and the army, who complained about being forced to cross the island to St George's. The convicts built St Peter's in a mock Byzantine style, copying the 12th century, at a cost of £2,400. It stand on the inland edge of the prison complex. Other civilising features followed, notably the erection of gas lights in The Grove in 1876. Inside, the prison had been lit from its own gas works from the time the first convicts arrived.

The prison became popular amongst visitors, awaiting the sight of work gangs being led to the quarries. The occasional escaper provided a little excitement in island life, like 33-year-old William Keagh (described as "a notorious burglar") who slipped away from one of the gangs on 5 December 1887 but was captured the following day in the harbour master's store at Castletown. It was the prison's boast that all who got away were recaptured.

In 1894 the Portland Breakwater scheme resumed. The plan now was to completely encircle the entire harbour. The advent of the torpedo boat had brought 20th century worries into naval thinking. There were already fears of sudden gunboat attacks and Portland's harbour works, conceived as protection against the weather, were now seen to be inadequate as a defence for the Fleet at anchor.

Only extended breakwaters could make the harbour safe. As it happened the navy was almost right. Torpedoes were to become the principal weapon against shipping, though they were mainly to come not from the surface but from a perfected form of "submersible".

The decision to enclose the whole of Portland Harbour was nothing if not ambitious. Two additional arms of the breakwater, making landfall halfway between Sandsfoot Castle and the Nothe Fort at Weymouth, would enclose four square miles of deep water.

When the second stage of the scheme was officially declared complete in 1903, it gave Portland one of the largest man-made harbours in the world. The area sealed off by the four lengths of breakwater is large enough to contain the harbours of Malta and Gibraltar, plus Hyde Park and Kensington Gardens. Upkeep was a problem from the start. Even in the year of so-called completion the new breakwater needed repairs after being battered by the sea in a gale on 12 December 1903. Bincleaves Groyne, at the Weymouth end, remained unfinished for several years; water lapped over it on the highest tides.

The Admiralty quarries were eventually to have their own railway network, with rolling-stock hauled by saddle-tank steam engines, which then meant that at the turn of the century Portland had four different railway systems – the original Merchants' stone line; the Admiralty Incline; the 1865

island branch line; and the quarry mineral lines. Now it has none.

The quarry system is best remembered for a dramatic accident in which the prison's own saddle-tank locomotive slid down a scree slope in what is now the Stadium area. Portland's historic cable-operated incline railway, lowering the stone on to the quay at Castletown, had its own mini-disaster on 15 June 1904.

Four loaded stone wagons ran away and left the track, crashing through the Admiralty slaughterhouse. The damage cost £300 to repair. The year 1904 marked the completion of modern Portland and most of its labour force was withdrawn. The "Mission to Navvies" closed.

The facts in this account have been checked and corrected by E. A. Andrews of 26 Channel View Road, Easton, who points out that the problem with much of what has been written about Portland is "that it is incorrect in a lot of detail". This will explain the differences between my text and that of others – this version is more likely to be correct!

Portland masons – for great work in Portland stone you visit London. There were few, if any, masons working on the island until the cutting of the railway in 1826 from the top of Verne down to the stone-quay at Castletown. Previously stone transported by sea was always cut at its destination. Later, in 1851, there were only thirty-three masons on the island, mostly working for the Admiralty in the construction of the breakwater.

Portland megaliths – nowhere in the books and reports on Dorset archaeology have I found mention of the impressive megalithic monuments surviving on Portland until the 1870s. A stone circle stood on the central northern top of the island, between Priory Corner and Easton, on ground undisturbed by quarrying.

From contemporary descriptions it appears to have been similar to the Bronze Age circles of sarsen stones on the downland between Dorchester and Bridport, and not unlike the numerous prehistoric stone circles of Dartmoor.

Clara King Warry, writing in 1920, recalled the Portland circle: "More than half a century ago, when the upland opposite the Saw Mill tavern on the western side of Easton Lane was all but intact, several yards inland from the high road was a group of large stones, some few erect, and the remainder lying in disorder on the ground. These possessed an attraction for me impossible to analyse, and I could rarely pass them without lingering a few moments."

Other stones lay about the Portland fields before the quarries were opened. Many must have been uncovered or moved by agricultural operations, but some of the arrangements do not sound natural. A second stone circle is said to have stood near the Saw Mill Tavern, to the east of the road, but not far away.

The most persistent of the stories of Portland's lost megalithic monuments concern the region around The Grove, before the convict prison was built. "The Druids put them there," said one local. "I've been told they were heathen temples, and that there were human sacrifices." The Grove, having such a suitable Druidic name, was the perfect place for such legends, and one stone was preserved by the prison builders but as it was moved the archaeological context was destroyed. No accurate description seems to survive of what actually stood at The Grove. One stone circle is claimed, but it seems there were a number of individual standing stones as well.

Portland's largest megalith, however, is said to have lain at a spot with the most descriptive place-name of all – Longstone Ope. "Longstone" is a name found in several places in Britain, and refers in these other cases as well to a fallen prehistoric menhir. All the Portland descriptions fall in well with what one expects of Bronze Age stone monuments, particularly the account of the circle near Easton Lane, and an additional

Portland quarries: seen in section at Easton, and with stone being loaded (opposite) on to a fleet of traction engines.

remark that only two or three of the stones were still upright. Some field names on old tithe and enclosure maps may give further clues to their location.

Before the hilltop at Verne was cut with the vast Victorian war-works, which included the ditch, ramparts and raking batteries of an underground fort, it was common land and covered with grass. There is no record of any megaliths there, but at the highest point (given as 499 feet above sea level on old maps) stood a cairn of stones. This

may have been an ancient burial mound. Close by were the stone-walled ruins of a small house and garden, surrounded by the double ramparts of an Iron Age hill-fort.

Portland Museum – Avice's Cottage, the picturesque thatched corner house at the south end of Wakeham, Portland, opened its doors to the public in 1930 (SY 697 713). Previously derelict, it had been given to the island by birth control advocate Dr Marie Stopes.

It has since expanded into a wholly admirable collection, spilling over into the next-door thatched cottage and out across the courtyard into a new gallery. Prize exhibits include Portland reeve staffs, markings on which record rents collected on behalf of the Court Leet, fern-tree fossils and numerous relics of quarrying and shipwreck.

That harsher side of life is accentuated by leg-irons and metal flails from Portland Prison. These put a double edge of strength and pathos along the blade of Portland history.

A display of condoms belongs in the 21st century but meanwhile there should be fuller acknowledgement of the foresight of Marie Stopes, to put her museum-creating into a wider context.

Portland Port – operating name of the new company formed by Langham Industries and Portland Development Partners, which acquired 350 acres of dockyards and adjacent land and breakwaters from the Ministry of Defence [1995].

It paid £2 million and announced plans for a roll-on roll-off ferry terminal; against a counter bid from Roil (UK) for a marine disposal centre at the former Royal Navy dockyard.

Portland quarries: retired steam engine, beside the eastern approach to Southwell in 1990.

Portland quarries: St Paul's Cathedral is a grand example of an end-user.

Portland quarries – see entry for **Quarries**.

Portland Raised Beach – 200,000-year-old geological rarity with exposures at Portland Bill, particularly on the western side of the Ministry of Defence compound, visible both inside the security fence and emerging on to the cliffs at the west and towards Pulpit Rock in the south (SY 676 684). This is a consolidated ancient beach. Once at sea level, it is now a platform 30 feet above the highest tides.

It comprises pebbles, stones, gravel, shells and sand fused into a calcareous mass by constant weathering. This under-layer is about 5 feet thick and covered by a wind-deposited stratum of orange sandy silt, about 6 feet in depth. Above this comes a deep brown solifluction deposit, a couple of feet thick, which was formed during the last major glacial period, the Devensian.

Portland Ribbon Wave – it says something for the climate of Portland and Torbay that they have the only British colonies of *Sterrha degeneraria*. This moth is only otherwise known from central Europe. Its British food plant is unknown.

Portland Roads – anchorage between Weymouth and Portland (SY 690 760) now enclosed by Portland Harbour [1847-1901]. As a patch of semi-open sea, sheltered from south-westerly winds, it frequently hosted the British fleet and was a life-saver for vessels that managed to escape treacherous conditions in Lyme Bay.

"I have seen some sixty to seventy vessels riding out a storm in Portland Roads, with more joining them by the hour," merchant seaman Joseph Red told the Commission of Enquiry into Harbours of Refuge [1844]. "My experience of 30 years has borne this out in each south-westerly gale."

The Royal Navy returned to Portland Roads after destroying Louis XIV's war-works and shipping in Cherbourg [7 August 1758], as did some vessels that took part in a social visit to mark the peace, more than a century later [15-17 August 1865].

Naval vessels stood offshore during many of King George III's frequent visits to Weymouth. He was taken on cruises, such as to Lulworth Cove, in vessels like the 32-gun HMS *Southampton* and 74-gun HMS *Magnificent*.

Warships have been an almost continuous sight since arrival of the first Royal Navy training ship [1862] though the dockyard is being run-down at the close of the 20th century.

Portland Sheep: a ram in the care of the Rare Breeds Survival Trust.

Portland Sago or Arrowroot – derivatives of *Arum neglectum* which is similar in basic appearance to the common Cuckoo-pint but grows much more lushly and to twice the height. The roots are edible if properly treated and were grown for this purpose on Portland in the 18th century, being marketed as Portland Arrowroot. It was a common starch and also had cosmetic uses for women – being said to remove freckles.

In its raw stage the plant is hardly that benign. Used as a medicinal herb it is potentially poisonous and was used against ring-worm and as a violent purgative.

Portland Sheep – are an exceptional rare breed. They used to be esteemed as a delicacy, extolled by some for the best mutton in England, but from a peak of 3,000 animals on the island in the early 19th century they dwindled to a flock of zero by the mid-20th century. That would have been extinction but for a few that found their way on to mainland farms; their descendants were reintroduced to the island in 1977 through the efforts of the Rare Breeds Survival Trust and Portland Field Research Group.

They graze the short turf around the Admiralty Underwater Weapons

Establishment beside an approach road to Portland Bill. The paucity of the island's flora, or rather its miniaturisation caused by the combination of a thin soil upon a rock that stands in the English Channel, no doubt accounts for their smallness. They weigh only about seventy pounds. This in turn enhances the taste, a fine-flavoured mutton, but their coats are minimal, with short, fine wool. The other characteristics are yellowish legs and a black nose.

The breed in its heyday was described by William Stevenson for the Board of Agriculture in 1811: "... there is a very small breed of sheep, and there are a few of the same kind at Studland, but they are not kept generally. They are said by many to be the true Dorsetshire breed ... The Dorset sheep, when compared with such as are at present kept in the Isle of Portland, will weigh three times as much; and it is not to be wondered at, as it may be observed that there are 3,000 sheep kept on the Island, which contains but 2,800 acres, of which 800 are waste, 400 arable, 250 meadow, which leaves 1,350 acres of pasture for the sheep, and this is very poor land, rented at 7s an acre."

In all probability Stevenson's informants were right and the Portland sheep are the direct descendants of the breed that was grazing not only Portland but southern England generally in Iron Age and Roman times. There were 900 sheep on the island when the Domesday Book was compiled in 1086. Today's animals are recorded in a "Flock Book" which was opened in 1974 to ensure that the strain remains pure. Each sheep carries an ear-tag with its number.

Portland Spies – known Soviet penetration of the top secret Underwater Weapons Establishment centres on the case that Lord Parker, the Lord Chief Justice, brought to its conclusion in the Old Bailey [22 March 1961].

Stocky, 39-year-old Gordon Lonsdale, "whose true identity may never be known," was the Russian agent who had tried to obtain the ultra secret of the Cold War. In this, we presume, he failed, in that we have been reassured that no British hunter-killer nuclear submarine, or one carrying ballistic missiles, was ever tracked while on patrol.

That said, it is conceded they had open access to a wealth of lesser value information about the new HMS *Dreadnought*, and were compromised by their own complacency rather than exposed by MI5 vigilance.

Lonsdale, whose real name was Colonel Conon Trifomovich Molody [born 1921], pretended to be a Canadian businessman. In 1960, disenchanted Colonel Michal Goleniewski, of the Polish

DAILY EXPRESS

No. 18,917   THURSDAY MARCH 23 1961   Weather: Cloudy; bright periods   Price 3d.

LONSDALE	KROGER	HIS WIFE	HOUGHTON	GEE	
25 years	20 years	20 years	15 years	15 years	PAGES 6, 7, 8

SPY RING CRUSHED

Lonsdale's identity still a riddle

By ARNOLD LATCHAM

THE dangerous career of the Russian agent who called himself Gordon Lonsdale, the "directing mind" of the Weymouth naval spies, ended at the Old Bailey yesterday with a sentence of 25 years' jail.

Stocky, 39-year-old Lonsdale, whose true identity may never be known, faced Lord Parker, the Lord Chief Justice, with a smile on his face, a flush on his cheeks, and the fading words of his counsel in his ears: "At least it can be said of this man that he was not a traitor to his own country."

But at the tone of Lord Parker's voice the smile vanished and he paled.

A gasp broke the silence of the packed court at the sentence—the longest passed there in memory.

He staggers backwards

Then it was the turn of the American-born Krogers —tall silver-haired 56-year-old Peter Kroger and his 47-year-old wife Helen, her lipstick smudged, her face sickening and ageing. For them, **20 YEARS** each.

When Colonel Abel, the Russian atom spy-master in the United States was arrested by G-men in 1957 photographs of the Krogers were found in his brief-case.

Peter Kroger, of Russian parentage, and Helen Kroger, from a Polish family real names Morris and Lona Cohen—came to England in 1954.

In the dock yesterday Kroger staggered backwards, brow creased to pain at the prospect of a near lifetime parting from his wife after 20 years of marriage.

Two warders crossed his arms but he reeled out to them in his wife's direction.

At the other end of the glass panelled dock, black-haired Harry Houghton Qate the old naval spy saboteur and servant spy. and his Mary secret, you silent

She held a folded sheet of paper in the folds of that dock and just down to write it with a that she's-a-spy, you enclosed from the Lonsdale and the Krogers.

Trembling

Lord Parker turned to Harry Houghton the ex-Navy master of arms, who passed in the service his Barrow wine.

Houghton, stooping and grey, and trembling, studied the old man, who was Reborn Spy.

Once 19 years. Lord Parker told him—because you do an old man it is not for the protection.

Houghton, has to listen. He may shorten from the old court hand he get out real also ind not word to him no dock. Boxierty 11 YEARS.

Lord Parker proceeded to whee Houghton and his Love his former partner Ethel Gee—now Miss Elizabeth Gee—aged 46.

With hands in her overcoat pockets and eyes down at bet in her dock.

But the sample of an early—15 YEARS.

But then for good "We have to give you ought your lose Love. Gee in the spy-master you-and passed to Lonsdale.

Lord Parker emphasised for when Houghton said You so dead he gave

↦ PAGE TWO, COL ONE

POCKET CARTOON

By OSBERT LANCASTER

"It's the Foreign Office—they want to know whether that prophetic times even you told them at the time of Burgess and Maclean?"

That £24,000 job —by union chief

A complaint up the subject of the new £24,000 a job for which the union chief made. position the Officer's new having financial the R-week and the £6 it when was.

So as it Lord Privy has reddened out how by at any job. for the up he in was, 'a weekly it the new to

The former and Lord Privy should be next out of said private subject I shall out not—

THE MAN WHO HUNTED SPIES ALONE

Three words and a hunch started the long trail of clues

By PERCY HOSKINS

Fred Hosking ... his suspicions sparked the spy hunt

THE sign of the swastika on an anonymous letter and the brilliant undercover work of a dockyard policeman started the Portland secrets case.

For six weeks Fred Hosking, 40 - year - old Admiralty constable who Britain's lone spy-catcher—

He relaxed none after hands gained to plans, pictures filed in a picture and Daily took a-house put chunk J. helped to set 1d.15 on a a message trail.

A grudge

One anonymous some months ago a real servant found a letter in to he den in the Underwater Weapons Establishment had quarters.

On it a pages sheet of dockyard notepaper was cross. Swastika in looking out with the words Too No one comes It of day the anti a reason Also it not heads took the letter to his chief and

The spy agents also a not heads took the letter to his desk upper office of Constable Hosking sped and in Establishment.

Hosking's the his short of spy he's a personal cipher crossed upper Barry Houghton.

He noticed his own Russell car He went dockyard workers he would doubt Housing of be but Houghton Barrow the-by tops... Housing's it was found on living-house spending a let on drink

And on man secretly mowered in Houghton's office in London Arch It no door who was a spy with and secret's at the Goldette of Weapons Establishment.

Every evening at 5.30 the full fatherly dedicatory gentleman brushed to his career home in home and waited on his distance.

In May it was reason for his church and for MI.5 and the spy hunt which was in can see men who months began a dossier.

The commands that started a faded out of the picture. He was not taking a grey erridonte at the Old Bailey. His were bear evidence that He-evidence Hocking can sock in the matter.

Major Bill tames his last bomb

Major Bill Barney aged 36, the Army's expert bomb-disposal expert, yesterday tackled his last unexploded mine. A 2,000lb monster he-a world- war II German bomb. Major Barney, who retires on April 28 spent five hours getting car bomb and said: I'm here. once my more the that.

Bus firms agree to new talks

Representatives of the 71 pro-vincial bus companies threatened with a bus strike agreed last night to resume talks with the union. The employers would only say that acceptance further strike notice had been received unions' Today when the employers made new offer.

ROYAL JOCKEY BREAKS BONES IN FALL

By CHARLES BENSON

ROYAL jockey Harry Carr was thrown heavily yesterday at the 31 runners in the Lincoln- shire Handicap charged for the winning post.

He lay still for some minutes while his wife, in the hospital where it was hoped that he would remain a ridden, rose and his small room in the race made

Carr's 20 1 mount, Road Race, fell about two furlongs from home.

He brought down another runner, Prince—Stone Jockey Keith Trople-hold and Kimber- with a neverbreak with several injuries third fourth

Badly shaken

At the inquest. Mrs Joan Carr racing two horses would last remained was X-rayed and was shaken.

Later he was advised to make one previous trip to his home in Newmarket by car.

Bad Mrs Carr I didn't see the accident but I was on the bottom step of the stand. But everyone around me said Road Race had fallen.

Waiting for race to be broadcast she added

He has told me that a horse ran across his mouth and brought him. As the time he ran fourth and he sent he had a good chance of winning

With that final beaten that it's a mistake he was fall most seriously

GRAND NATIONAL HOPES Badness and Sea Fund a I man to never against the Aintree course. Owner and Stone's action three Bucket by Aintree

He did said Bossanova Frost I'll-I can have a horse against his National no I may be broadside or his Saturday

Six-shooter riddle

A trace of glint was sifting out I am for the rumours of 15 peace plates from a Southgate London area of gun dealers

Gun owner is that the is-they were rumbles who drew WM9 What sire and I wanted has plastics I complete their revolver current.

MPs to quiz Premier on secrets

THE secrets trial will be referred to in the Commons today when to god to the Prime Minister Mr Harold Macmillan a nominal head of security in Britain.

Mr Lambeth Leader of the Opposition may propose that a high level inquiry be set up to make more sure that military secrets cannot be transmitted to any other country.

Foundry blast injures 12   Kitchen explosion kills wife

Britain gets tough over Laos

By DOUGLAS CLARK

A SOLEMN warning to the Soviet Government on the deteriorating position in Laos was in the hands of the British ambassador in Moscow, Sir Frank Roberts, last night for delivery at the earliest opportunity.

If the prospect of another Korea will loom closer with American and even British troops liable to intervene directly in this far-off civil war.

The British Note, I under-stand, will tell Mr Krush-chev that unless he works positively towards a cease fire, then responsibility for whatever follows including a possible extension of the conflict—will rest with him.

The warning is being sent by Britain before than America became Britain in conjunction with Russia of the 1954 Geneva Conference which invited the Indo-China war.

INSPIRATION

But by inspiration comes from President Kennedy who has told Britain agreeably that he wants than in Laos as Communist set-up.

The Tone of Laos, he fire ago'd would evoke America's position in the Far East beyond his acquisition 1950

Washington fears that militarily forces are now be had in Laos that its capital Vientiane could fall to the rebels at any moment.

Britain is now certain that he position is so desperate in this Red-Pretext.

IAN SMEY in Washington reports: President Kennedy is anxious that the Laotian crisis is a nationwide interests and radio stations

He explained to say that the United States is not prepared to rush arms and military hardware to Laos in a crisis on a ballot he never has against a Soviet arms airlift to Indo-China route.

Makarios: I will quit

Archbishop Makarios President of Cyprus, said before flying home from London yesterday that he will give up his politics.

"After independence I announced that the people of Cyprus needed my services and than I could not stay," he said.

"However, I have an intention of giving up the political power. I will serve says her the first period."

LATEST

KIDNAPPED BOY FOUND DEAD
See Page Four
BELLEVILLE, Ontario, Wednesday.—Thomas McMartIn, 10-year-old kidnapped boy was found dead, police reported.

★ ★

FLEet-street 8000

this marriage was arranged

Swallow here married up the last friend of Tarylene with a new alley being that is washable and grandply. The partnerbody's perfect and makes a romance you will not only full far we eight, but will find so simple to keep impeccably good-looking. In the shops NOW. in fashionable styles in fashionable shades. Man's from £9.9.0. Ladies' from £7.9.0

French cut tariffs by 5 per cent

PARIS, Wednesday. France is to cut another figure in fine her own from April 1 it is understood. The cut continues the five per cent reduction this year.

Portland Spies: their last day in court.

Intelligence Service, told the CIA that British anti-submarine defences were being revealed to the Russians. Already, in the autumn of 1959, Detective Constable Leonard Burt of Weymouth police heard that Admiralty clerk Harry Houghton, "who worked at the nearby Portland naval base, with access to secret material, was regularly visiting the Polish Embassy in London".

Houghton's profligacy on a £14-a-week salary included sustained drinking bouts with Admiralty records office clerk Ethel "Bunty" Gee. Both were now under police surveillance, with sightings of Houghton and his new off-white Renault Dauphine being communicated under the code-word "Off-White" in case radio frequencies were being monitored.

There was also "a fatherly dockyard policeman" on the case inside the Underwater Weapons Establishment: "For six weeks Fred Hosking, 60-year-old Admiralty constable, was Britain's lone spy-chaser." A civil servant had found a letter on his desk: "On a single sheet of notepaper, scrawled by brush in tracing ink, were the words 'You dirty Jew'. In one corner was daubed a black swastika."

Constable Hosking was handed the letter by the recipient, who was not Jewish, with the information that the culprit was Houghton, "a man he knew bore

him a personal grudge".

The net tightened as it was realised that Harry Houghton had a regular pattern of visiting London, on the first Saturday of each month. Intelligence officers watched as Houghton and Gee handed a bag to a man near Waterloo Station. That man was Gordon Lonsdale, who MI5 investigator William "Jim" Skardon traced to a Ruislip bungalow that was the home of Helen and Peter Kroger.

Lonsdale and the Krogers were now at the centre of an MI5 operation, being observed by a travelling circus of phoney door-to-door salesmen, gardeners, and telephone engineers.

The trap was sprung outside the Old Vic Theatre on one of Houghton's Saturday visits to London [7 January 1961]. Lonsdale's pockets were stuffed with bank notes. Houghton was accompanied by Gee, whose basket of cheap groceries covered the real shopping. Microfilm contained 310 classified photographs of Admiralty documents, including construction details of HMS *Dreadnought*.

Meanwhile, the Krogers were also about to be arrested, though neither MI5 nor Special Branch held any clue as to their real identities. Peter Kroger traded as an antiquarian bookseller from 190 The Strand, specialising in "Americana from the North Pole to the South Pole" and travelled to book fairs across

Europe. This gave him respectable international credentials though he enjoyed a seedier side line in pornography. "Books with microdots," Skardon quipped.

He found, inside their Ruislip bungalow, a cache of cloak-and-dagger accessories. The tin of Yardley Invisible Talc contained hidden compartments. A hip flask had its secret insert for sprinkling iron oxide on magnetic tape, in order to read Morse code. A tin of face powder incorporated a microdot reader. The refrigerator concealed a short-wave radio – another was missed by MI5 and dug up in the garden by new owners years later [1977]. There was a Minox camera and £6,000 cash. Classified documents spilled out of books and from beneath floorboards.

"At least it can be said of this man that he was not a traitor to his own country," Lord Parker said as he sent Lonsdale down for 25 years. He sentenced the Krogers to 20 years each and Houghton and Gee to 15 years apiece.

Only when Peter Kroger's photograph was spotted by an American journalist did MI5 realise that they had been watching the most successful partnership in espionage history. Helen and Peter, as Lona and Morris Cohen, were FBI-listed "missing persons" who disappeared just before Ethel and Julius Rosenberg, run by Russian master-spy Colonel Rudolf Abel, were arrested [1950]. Cohen had founded the ring that included agent "Perseus" whose information enabled the Soviet Union to develop and explode an atomic bomb [1948].

Lonsdale would be swapped for British spy Greville Wynne [1964] and the Krogers were exchanged even more unequally [1969] for Gerald Brooke, whose offence had been to distribute anti-Communist leaflets in Moscow. Houghton and Gee were released from prison shortly afterwards.

Helen Kroger [1913-92] and Peter Kroger [1910-95] settled in the Soviet Union and moved close to Helen's family home, living at Lublin on the Polish border.

Speculation continues that there was another Portland spy who escaped detection when MI5 Director-General Sir Roger Hollis discontinued investigations. Sir Roger himself emerged as the prime suspect for the security service's own "undiscovered mole" in Peter Wright's *Spycatcher* [1987].

Portland stone – see entries for **Quarries** and **Stone trade**.

Portland Stonecrop – identified as such by botanist and royalist Colonel Thomas Johnson [died 1644] who revised and expanded *The Herball ... gathered by John Gerarde* [1633]: "There is a plant called *Sedum Portlandicum*, or Portland Stonecrop, of the English Island called Portland, lying on the South coast, having goodly branches and a rough rind. The leaves imitate *Laureola* (Laurel). It grows among the Tithymales (spurges; *Euphorbias* species) but is thicker, shorter, more fat and tender. The stalk is of a woody substance like *Laureola*." He goes on to say it is also reminiscent of *Crassula*, *Sempervivum* and Tithymales, and concludes somewhat uncertainly that "it shall be less prejudicial to the truth to account it as a shrub degenerating from both kinds".

Botanists continue to debate the point, with the favourite being *Sedum praealtum* 'Cristatum' though *Sedum reflexum* 'Monstrosum Cristatum' and *Aeonium arboreum* 'Cristatum' also have their supporters. Given the quantity of the unidentified plants on the Portland cliffs one would have thought the argument would have been settled generations ago.

Potter – authoress **Beatrix Potter** [1858-1943] took her father to see Portland on 11 April 1895 but saw no point in going again: "Portland Island is a curiosity to see once. Very like Gibraltar only flat-topped.

Steamship 'Preveza': Greek vessel washed into Chesil Cove, 1920.

Pulpit Rock: Dorset's southern tip.

The top is one vast quarry and stony wilderness. The convicts did not particularly appeal to me."

Pressgang massacre – see **Easton Pond Massacre**.

Preveza – Greek steamship driven ashore in Chesil Cove [15 January 1920]. Her boilers would lie on the shingle for more than a decade.

Prisons – confusingly, the Victorian Convict Prison at The Grove is now the Young Offenders' Institution, and the fortifications at Verne Citadel have become a Home Office Prison.

See entries for **Portland convict poem**, **Forger's Slate**, **Portland Harbour**, **Verne Citadel**, *Weare* **prison ship**, and the **Young Offenders' Institution**.

Providence Place – No 51 Weston Road, beside the narrow Gypsy Lane which led into Verlands Lawnsheds from Weston Green (SY 687 712) is one of the best late-Tudor houses on the island. Previously half of a double pair – the matching left-hand half continuing at the gable end – it is a thatched one-and-a-half storeys with high attic rooms.

Pulpit Rock – famous feature of Portland Bill, created about 1875 when quarrymen working the adjoining Beacon Quarry left a chunk of cliff standing proud from the ledges of their working floor (SY 676 683).

Q

Quarries – for the island's monument look around you, but preferably when you are in London. What the quarrylands have done to Portland itself is truly monumental in scale but hardly architectural in detail. There are, however, enough discarded blocks of semi-cut stone and inland cliffs gouged out of the rock to show the link between the island and the capital. Less attractive are the half-hearted attempts at filling holes in the ground which generally degenerate into a surface clutter of discarded cars and mattresses.

Past and present quarries cover half the island. The entire northern top was once quarried, from the string of workings along the top of West Weares – Tout, Inmosthay, Trade and Bower's Quarries – which are still romantic with the great scree-slopes of waste slipping three hundred feet from the edge of West Cliff down to the water at Clay Ope. Along the top there is a coastal path from Priory Corner (SY 685 729) that follows the course of the 19th century horse-drawn tramway under neat little bridges that carried the spoil trucks above it to the tipping points on the edge.

A much bleaker landscape, with great open areas of nothing, characterises the eastern top, from the viewpoint car-park at Waycroft Quarry (SY 691 731) on Verne Yeates to King Barrow, Admiralty, Withies Croft and the Independent Quarries. No better are the old Prison/Borstal complex above the incline that took the stone down to the former King's Pier below East Weares (SY 702 734). These are High Headlands, France, Broadcroft, Yeolands and Silklake Quarries.

South of the hilltop communities, the overgrown villages of Weston and Easton, lie Bottom Combe, Perryfield, Grangecroft and Suckthumb Quarries. The workings from Church Ope Cove to Cave Hole, along the lower south-eastern cliffs, are known as Sheat Quarry. Inland, south of Southwell village, there are quarries on Langley Hill. Finally, the south-western extremity of the island has the smallest but best known of the island's workings, Beacon Quarry, which extends from Portland Bill across to inside the Admiralty radar compound security fence.

Rev John Skinner [1772-1839] of Camerton, near Bath, describes in his journal the pre-mechanisation methods of hauling stone on Portland: "... large hewn stones lie scattered in all directions; indeed the quarries worked on the island are prodigious and the mode of conveying the ponderous masses down the steep slopes unavoidably arrests the attention of the stranger. The blocks being placed on a strong wooden carriage with solid wheels apportionate to the weight they are to sustain, two horses are harnessed on before and one and sometimes two behind, the latter being supplied with strong breaching, in order to act as drawbacks to the carriage, and prevent it running with too great velocity down the steep incline. Indeed the sagacity and exertions of these poor animals in this very arduous employment is really astonishing; they squat down on their haunches and suffer themselves to be dragged for many yards, struggling with all their strength against the weight that forces them forward. To one unaccustomed to the sight it appears as though their limbs must inevitably be dislocated or their sinews cracked by the violence of their exertions. Indeed one compassionates these poor creatures the rather, as all this labour might easily be obviated by the simple construction of a railroad" [which was to take place in 1862].

Portland stone came to fame before Christopher Wren rebuilt fifty churches and other public buildings following the Great Fire – the conflagration that destroyed London in 1666.

John Denham, who succeeded Inigo Jones as the king's surveyor of buildings in 1643, travelled down to Dorset but the visit coincided with his "distemper of madness", John Aubrey records, "when he went from London to see the famous freestone quarries at Portland in Dorset, and when he came within a mile of it, turned back to London again, and did not see it". He may have been put off by the ferry at the Small Mouth crossing point.

The mid-20th century decline of the quarries has now stabilised. Most of the orders for proper building stone are for repairs to major prestigious frontages. The return to traditional architectural values has brought Portland stone back to the City if not to the high streets. For all that, the bulk of the stone that leaves Portland is crushed rock, but the main markets for this are in south-east England and high transport costs do not allow Portland's products to be delivered at a competitive price. Noise and dust are no longer taken for granted as they once were, and quarry proposals for land near residential areas – or on scenic cliffsides – have been rejected. The industry, at one time the island's major employer, has been reduced to a hundred men.

A working party advised in the 1970s that its only practical hope for an improved future lies in a proposal to build a deepwater quay on the east side of the island. This would enable the stone to be shipped out, as was always the historical practice, at economic rates. Shipping costs are so much lower than road haulage rates, particularly for heavy loads over long distances. It has been estimated for example that if the Severn tidal barrage is ever built it would be less expensive to bring in stone by sea from North Africa than by road from the nearby Mendip quarries. Whether Portland ever has its own quay again is going to depend upon the attitude of the Ministry of Defence, who insist that nothing can be allowed to interfere with access into Portland Harbour.

There matters rest for the time being. On one side the local authorities are insisting upon a wider "green margin" around all residential areas, "to ensure that quarrying takes place further from houses than it can and does now". They have also demanded that rights of way are protected: "The past practice of quarrying away paths, and applying for formal closures or diversions afterwards, must cease."

Expansion, on the other hand, depends upon demand. Aggregates, it might be argued, are a waste and squandering of the assets of Portland. They call for the crushing of one of the finest building stones in Europe. They do not proffer much hope for local jobs either, as a council policy statement points out. For only the extraction of building stone can restore the quarries to a full level of work. "The traditional quarrying and masonry skills mean more for Portland employment than jobs in aggregate production."

R

Rabbit, taboo word – on Portland it is not used, though bunnies or long-ears are acceptable. I haven't tried the mediaeval word, coneys, on the natives. This cannot be a superstition dating back to Celtic times, as rabbits were not introduced to Britain until the 12th century, but beliefs of ill-omen may have transferred to it from hares, which were sacred to the Celts. Anyway, it was considered extremely unlucky, and not just on Portland, for a fisherman to encounter a rabbit whilst going to his boat, or for a miner to come across one while on the way to the pit. Boating and mining were Portland's main trades so the superstition was doubly relevant here.

Kingsley Palmer writes in *Oral Folk Tales of Wessex*, 1973: "There is a story that the rabbits could cause a great deal of damage with their burrows, thus rendering the quarries unsafe, and had been the cause of more than one fatal accident. While this may be partly true, the rabbit may have had some significance in pagan lore that is still partly remembered."

His latter suggestion is, however, nonsense as the rabbit was not found in Britain until its introduction by the Normans. The similar creature of real Celtic associations is the hare but that is ground-living and hardly a hazard to the quarrymen. As "cony" or "coney" – from its name in Old French – the rabbit occurs as the basis for local place names all over Dorset.

Taboo words are, however, very much avoided in other parts of Britain. On a television report I heard a woman describing how her daughter died in a community close to Sellafield nuclear re-processing plant, Cumbria: "It was cancer but we managed to keep that quiet for more than a year, because of the stigma."

The Race – shallow, turbulent waters frothing off Portland Bill (SY 677 681) caused by contra-flows in the tide and the sheer volume of water displaced southwards by the project of the Isle of Portland and Weymouth peninsula, eight miles into the English Channel.

Railway – the former line from Weymouth to Portland was built between 1862-64 as a joint venture between the Great Western Railway

Portland Railway: with a train midway between the island and the mainland, seen from the site of Whitehead Torpedo Works at Wyke Regis.

and the London and South Western Railway. It ran beside the sea for two miles. A row over the management of Weymouth station delayed its opening till October 1865.

The Small Mouth had been bridged by a timber viaduct and the line was double gauged with three rails to take the 7 feet wheelspan of GWR trains. In 1903 the wooden viaduct was replaced by a steel structure.

The line went through an optimistic stage in the 1930s and Sandsfoot Castle Halt was opened.

From then it was in decline. Passenger services ended in 1952 – though there was the Queen's train on 29 April 1959 – and the last goods wagons were taken out on 9 April 1965. The Fleet viaduct was demolished in 1971 and the dismantled line to Portland now

turns purple in summer with expanses of thrift.

Raised Beach – geological landform exposed at Portland Bill, from a time of higher sea-levels, lying across the ground as a composite aggregate of single, sand, and broken shells. Its most notable exposure is 12 feet deep. The "raised beach" epithet was coined by a Victorian geologist named Whitaker [1869].

Shells date the bed to 200,000 years of age. It is much like any fiercely pounded current beach in that it also contains fragments and larger pieces of erratic rock from far-flung deposits, brought by vigorous wave action, including quartzite, granite, and sarsen stone.

Rand – sailing ship wrecked in Chesil Cove, Chiswell [circa 1920].

Ranters' Lodge: with Joey Stone (left) and the Dead House (right).

Ranters' Lodge – next to the Dead House on the edge of Chesil Cove, Chiswell, with the gable end set towards the sea in a more conventional aspect, is another single-storey stone building (SY 683 733). This was the "Preaching Room" of the Primitive Methodists of Victorian times which was known to the rest of the population as the Ranters' Lodge. It, like the Dead House, had originally been built as a store for fishing tackle.

By 1869 most of the island's Primitive Methodists were using their purpose-built chapel which had been erected on Miser's Knap and which is now the Royal Manor Theatre. The Ranters' Lodge and its adjacent mortuary reverted to stores for fishing tackle. By 1945 they were being used by Joey Stone who had two hundred and fifty lobster pots and great lengths of heavy net which were draped over the old beams.

There was a sixty gallon copper, heated by a fire of the driftwood which was always appearing on the beach, on which the nets were *barked*. This was a dark-brown dyeing process that left the sides of the net visible to the fish to direct them into its hose.

Boys were employed to sit on the beach and cut *merks* which were the two pieces of cork that fitted each lobster pot. These also required beachtop maintenance, being rebound on the bottom and given new weights, before being dipped in boiling tar and then spread out across the pebbles in rows to dry. Each weighed 40lbs and they tended to take a battering from Portland's sliding pebbles and its hostile elemental forces. Some took hours to refurbish.

Offshore, the operation was handled by three Portland lerrets, the island's traditional rowing boat which was pointed at both ends and crewed by four or six men. Phyllis Ribbons has also recorded that Joey Stone had four pot-boats

Reeve Staff: symbols record the parish rents.

which had a square stern. His was the last major fishing industry on the Chesil Cove and three eras have closed upon these two stout little buildings.

HMS *Recoil* – Royal Navy armed trawler sunk by a German mine off Portland [28 September 1940]. A large explosion was heard but no wreckage or survivors were found.

Reeve Staff – pole of authority and record of the "Gerefa" or Reeve steward of the Court Leet of the Isle of Portland. Symbols notch-up the parish rates, with signs used for centuries, and perpetuate a system devised in Anglo-Saxon times. These represent the hamlets on the island, with knife-cuts to show the shillings and pence:

O	=	Southwell
x inside O	=	Wakeham
/x/	=	Weston
W	=	Easton
V	=	Chiswell
whole-notch	=	one shilling
half-notch	=	sixpence
full-scratch	=	penny
half-scratch	=	halfpenny
quarter-scratch	=	farthing
dots/cuts	=	separate individual sums

William White is the earliest known Reeve [1700] but the office and its poles date back to antiquity. Many of the old staffs survive. Most are in deal, but pine and mahogany were also used, and vary in length. The longest is 12 feet and has sides that are $1^1/_2$ inches square.

Reforne – the main east-west street in the centre of the island, leading from Easton Square (SY 692 718) to St George's Church (SY 687 720), giving its name to the district westwards of Easton. In the middle of its north side is Apsley House which has an 1815 datestone but the oldest dated building is the George Inn [1765] at the west end of the south side, beside Every's Close and the closest building to the church.

Several other older buildings incorporate 17th century walls but have been generally rebuilt or refronted.

The biggest public building, opposite the Police Station, was the National School built [1836] for 440 boys and girls by the National Society for Promoting the Education of the Poor in the Principles of the Established Church. The field behind it is known as Jordan.

Every's Close was dominated by a Coastguard Station, on the east side near the far end.

The oldest house in Reforne, to the west of the former railway bridge on the north side of the street is Apsley House, which has a Waterloo year datestone [1815].

South Portland Labour Club was established in Reforne [1888] and moved to the Coronation Hall in Moorfield Road, coinciding with a visit to Portland by King Edward VII [3 April 1902].

Reliance – a ketch shipwrecked on the east side of Portland Bill, when she was wedged into a cavern, snapping her main mast which was a foot in diameter [December 1949].

Rendel – engineer **James Meadow Rendel** [1799-1856] devised the method for building Portland Harbour, using timber scaffolding stretching outwards from the arm of the first breakwater, along which railway trucks could drop their stone vertically into the water.

The result would be the largest man-made harbour in the world, built in two phases [1849-72 and 1894-1903], which would turn Rendel's original Harbour of Refuge into 4 square miles of enclosed deep-water anchorage.

Resolution (prison ship) – see entry for **Weare**.

Ribbon Wave – see entry for **Portland Ribbon Wave**.

RNAL 50 – the Royal Navy Air Landing ship moored in Portland, used by aircrew and handling parties for practising deck landings. With more than 100,000 logged so far she has more landings and take-offs to her credit than any other vessel in the Royal Navy.

Roads – see entry for **Portland Roads** anchorage.

HMS *Rodney* – 33,900-ton battleship, carrying 16-inch guns, which sailed from Portland Harbour, escorted by the destroyers HMS *Jervis* and *Faulkner*, to bombard substantial German gun emplacements on the occupied Channel Island of Alderney [12 August 1944].

Roe – pioneer aviator **Humphrey Verdon Roe** [1878-1949], second husband of contraception advocate Dr Marie Stopes, lived at the Higher Lighthouse, Southwell, Portland. His autobiographical *Who's Who* entry explains how he came to make flying machines: "From 1909 onwards, when flying seemed to be a dream, his foresight and faith in its future led him to devote the whole of his capital and talents to helping his brother Sir Alliott Verdon-Roe, to establish the Avro biplane."

They founded plane-makers A. V. Roe and Company Limited. Humphrey left in 1917 to join the Royal Flying Corps, in France, and was wounded on active service [1918].

'Royal Adelaide': painting of the famous wreck of the Chesil Beach.

Royal Adelaide – the 1,385-ton sailing ship was outward-bound from London to Sydney, with a varied cargo that included emigrants for Australia, when she was driven broadsides on to the Chesil Beach, between Chiswell and Wyke Regis [25 November 1872].

Waves broke over the length of the vessel and surged high up the beach. Portlanders waded into the swell, their efforts illuminated by hand-held flares, and a rocket-fired line delivered a rope to the crew and passengers who had retreated to the stern. Sixty of them were saved by being strapped to life-saving apparatus and sent down the rope.

Then, tragically, this snapped and the remaining seven on board – who had been helping the others – were drowned.

Nonetheless, it was regarded as a miracle that any, let alone so many, had been saved. Portlanders received acclamation for their "prodigies of valour" and enjoyed the practical consolation that the ship soon broke-up and disgorged a cargo of spirits.

Royal Naval Air Station – flying Short-830 seaplanes, from Portland Harbour, a unit operated anti-submarine patrols over the English Channel during the final years of the Great War [1917-18]. Their hangar was erected immediately above the Target Slipway, between Camber Jetty and the Loading Jetty, with this slip being used for quick take-offs and recovery.

Recommissioned during the Cold War as Royal Naval Air Station, Portland [1959], for the anti-submarine helicopters of HMS *Osprey*, on a site west of Portland Castle, and later expanded across the reclaimed Mere (SY 682 743).

Wessex and Wasp helicopters would be followed by Sea King and Lynx. The airfield survived the closure of the adjacent naval base [1995] but is also expected to close by the end of the century.

Royal Reviews – the first great review of the Royal Navy at Portland, comprising the combined Home and Atlantic Fleets, was carried out by "Sailor King" George V [8-11 May 1912] soon after his accession. The first day's activities were cancelled by fog; indeed this caused the Royal Yacht and the King to arrive late from the Isle of Wight, and First Lord of the Admiralty Winston Churchill stood in for him on the previous day [7 May].

Political leaders were also present, headed by Liberal Prime Minister Herbert Asquith and the Conservative leader of the Opposition, Arthur Balfour. They were treated to some superlative gunnery from the battleships HMS *Orion* and HMS *Neptune*.

The Fleet outgrew Portland Harbour as it assembled for a Royal Review. Usually the ships would be gathered in a north-east to south-west grid that started at Bincleaves Groyne and extended the width of Weymouth Bay, with the inner line being small vessels such as minesweepers and motor-torpedo boats, extending seawards for two miles, into the open sea beyond the East Ship Channel of the harbour breakwaters.

King Edward VIII visited Portland to review 40 ships of the Home Fleet [12 November 1936]. It was to be the former naval cadet's first and last visit to the Fleet as monarch. His train arrived at Portland to a wild reception from the weather.

The train pulled into the station yard just before 04.30 hours in a full gale. A wave had broken over the Chesil Beach and flooded Castletown and Victoria Square, where the station yard was inundated and 2 feet of water surged beneath the royal train.

The King remained sleeping, however, until eight o'clock. The royal car had to force its way between floodwater and cheering children on its short route to the dockyard.

His Majesty embarked on the royal yacht *Victoria and Albert* to cross the turbulent waters to the warships at anchor. Twenty-one guns fired a salute across the water as the sun broke through.

The King's inspection was undertaken in the Commander-in-Chief's barge and he then lunched on the flagship HMS *Nelson*. In the evening he attended a concert party aboard the aircraft carrier HMS *Courageous,* followed by dinner on the royal yacht.

The following afternoon thousands of people lined the streets of Weymouth as the King drove to the main station to board a train for Paddington. This time the sun shone and he was given an enthusiastic reception. Mentally, however, he was preoccupied – a month later he would abdicate.

The next notable royal review [9 August 1939] was by his successor, King George VI, but the weather had hardly improved; neither had the political outlook. The Mayor of Weymouth apologised for the visibility across Weymouth Bay from Bincleaves Groyne, because most of the 120 ships of the Reserve Fleet were obscured by mist and drizzle.

"Don't worry, Mr Mayor," the King replied, "it's raining everywhere."

Rufus Castle – romantic ruin, otherwise known as Bow and Arrow Castle, perched on a precipice above Church Ope Cove, Portland (SY 696 791) with a squat, a roofless tower in the floor-plan of an irregular pentagon. This was built in the 15th century and has a 19th century gateway and bridge.

Rufus Castle: commanding view over the beachhuts of Church Ope Cove.

It is said to have been built on the site of an earlier castle, constructed in the time of William II [nicknamed King Rufus; reigned 1087-1100], that was captured by Robert, Earl of Gloucester, in 1142. The rebuilding was carried out by Richard, Duke of York, between 1432 and 1460.

S

Sago – see entry for **Portland Sago**.

St Andrew's Avalanche Memorial Church – a prim Victorian building at Southwell (SY 688 701) erected [1879], at a cost of £2,000, in commemoration and thanks for the saving by Portlanders, at great risk to two boat crews, of the twelve survivors of the collision south-west of Portland Bill between the Shaw Saville clipper *Avalanche*, carrying New Zealand emigrés, and the *Forest* of Windsor, Nova Scotia [11-12 September 1877].

One hundred and six drowned. "The interest excited by this awful disaster had been further increased by the discovery that only one of the ships sank after the collision," it was reported three days' later. "The hull of the *Forest* was visible from the Nothe and the Breakwater on Saturday. Apparently it had not shifted far from the Shambles lightship."

The following week, HMS *Defence*, an ironclad of the Channel Fleet, spent several days shelling and depositing kegs of explosive, with indifferent results, in attempts at sinking "this great towering hull, rising like a rock out of the sea."

Some of the bodies, including the *Avalanche's* carpenter, J. H. Jamieson, "AND FIVE OTHERS NAMES UNKNOWN" are buried in St George's churchyard. Others having been recovered from Chesil Cove. Others, however, were washed up miles from Portland, such as Robert Dudgeon, the 29-year-old ship's cook – named "Dundem", probably in error, on the Portland memorial plaque – who lies in the old churchyard at West Lulworth.

In 1984, divers from Bingham Sub-Aqua Club, Nottinghamshire, discovered the wreck of the Avalanche and brought up quantities of dinner service and other pottery, with the Shaw Saville crest. A representative collection is displayed in St Andrew's Church. Her anchor is now on the grass in front of the building.

John Callan of Southwell designed the commemorative stained glass window [1981].

St Andrew's Church – the ruin of Portland's mediaeval parish church stands in the only sheltered glade

St Andrew's (old): pointed arch over the path into the ruins.

that the island possesses, a gully that drops from Pennsylvania Castle to the sea at Church Ope Cove (SY 697 711). It was dedicated in 1475 and stood in the only tree-full place on this island, now mainly salt-tolerant sycamores, and looked much the same when the antiquary John Leland visited Portland in 1540: "There be very few or utterly no trees on the site, saving the elms about the church." He found the isle "very bleak".

The ruin of St Andrew's church has a pointed arched doorway, some walling of circa 1475, and gravestones with quarrying family names. The last recorded burial took place in 1752 and the building fell into complete disrepair in 1756 when it was abandoned in favour of the temporary Tabernacle and the new church of St George at Reforne. It had been agreed in 1753 that it was too small, in poor condition, liable to slip down the

St Andrew's (new):
the 1879 Avalanche
Memorial Church.

cliff, and in the wrong place for most of the island's population. A parish committee decided that it would be "imprudent for the inhabitants to put themselves to the expense of a thorough repair of the same, since it appears to us that such repairs must cost more than half the expense of building a new church".

Remains of earlier Saxon or Norman buildings have been found on the landslipped site of the former St Andrew's; its name has been transferred to church a new site at Southwell [1879].

St George's – the magnificent church at Reforne, which to Sir Nikolaus Pevsner was "the most impressive 18th century church in Dorset". It is at the edge of the quarrylands, in the centre of the exposed western top of the island (SY 686 720) and takes its name as much from the monarch as from the saint because George II, as Lord of the manor of Portland, gave the land and £500 towards its construction. This began in 1754.

Its builder, Thomas Gilbert, does not seem to have designed anything before but henceforth he would be rightly described as an "architect", not that he would benefit as he died in his moment of glory – almost as the church was being consecrated by the Bishop of Bristol [1766]. The clean-cut classical work is the best example of Portland stonework that you will find on the island. Its lines of box pews – it had to accommodate six hundred – are overlooked by the twin pulpit and the galleries.

That the Georgian elegance and the original pews survive is due to the lucky accident of Portland's unusual land-laws. Gavelkind was the custom of shared inheritance, the island's properties being passed on by equitable division among beneficiaries, and it also applied to the church pews. Freehold rights in these were split between the members of hundreds of island families so that when it was decided to modernise the seating it was found to be impossible to find and get the agreement of all the part-owners involved.

So St George's church was simply abandoned and a mock-15th century alternative, the church of All Saints, built half-a-mile to the east, in Easton, during the Great

St George's: Georgian masterpiece.

War. It was consecrated in 1917 and St George's was left in its magnificent time-warp. It and the surrounding headstones, the best collection of Georgian and Victorian churchyard monuments in Dorset, are now in the care of the Friends of St George's.

St John's Church – the Anglican church beside High Street, Fortuneswell (SY 687 736), built to the designs of Edward Mondey or Charles Wallis [1839-40]. With sittings for 616, it cost £2,115, plus £200 for the ground. The building is in Portland stone and dominated by a three-stage tower. The chancel and organ chamber were added later by George Crickmay [1876].

St Peter's Church – the "Convict Church" in The Grove, built for the use of the prisoners [1872]. They were its builders, with costs totalling £2,400 being met by public subscription, to provide for their "moral improvement".

The carvings are also the work of the convicts, and the mosaic floors

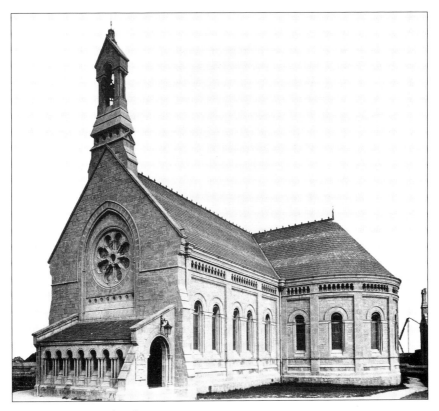

St Peter's: 'Convict Church'.

were laid by Constance Kent, who was convicted of murdering her stepbrother. Ceilings are in Finnish redwood, entirely assembled in pure tongued and grooved perfection, held with wooden pegs rather than nails.

A remarkable finishing touch, in the bell-cote, is a miniature carving of the church itself. Whatever qualities were lacking in the minds of Victorian prisoners their skills are inspirational.

The Salt Wreck – a French brigantine, captured by the *Crescent* frigate when she was sailing from Rochelle towards Rouen, was brought to Portland Roads as a prize in March 1793. She was laden with salt but the cargo would be lost when she dragged her anchor and was driven on shore beside Portland Castle. The ship suffered considerable damage but all the crew were saved.

Sapphire – coal-laden schooner wrecked in Chesil Cove [8 August 1883]. Her crew were rescued by rocket apparatus.

Sea creature legend – the story of the Portland cock, a fabulous maritime creature, was recorded by the chronicler Raphael Holinshed [died 1590] and repeated by county historian John Hutchins:

"In November 1457, in Portland, was seen a cock coming out of the sea having a great crest on its head, a great red beard, and legs half a yard long. He stood on the water and crowed three times, and every time turned himself about and beckoned with his head, north, south, and west. He was in colour like a pheasant, and when he had crowed he vanished."

The cock is strongly associated with the Romano-Celtic culture and was the subject of some charming little enamelled brooches, not that I am seriously suggesting a lingering folk memory in this case. It might more likely have started with the figure-head of a boat being seen after a wreck. Or, with greater probability, that the entire island population was drunk.

SDV mini-submarine – "a vessel of a classified nature" operated by the Special Boat Squadron, flooded on reversing and diving when coming too close inshore in Portland Harbour [April 1994]. Sergeant Richard Howard drowned as he removed his face mask at the moment his diving line to the craft was jerked underwater.

HMS *Sereptia* – Portland's Royal Navy shore-base, established in the Great War [1917].

The Shambles – offshore sandbank, east-south-east of Portland Bill, formerly marked by a

Lightship, and now an automatic buoy. The hazardous shoals were named for their shipwreck carnage, "Shambles" being a mediaeval butchery.

The Shambles is a bank of sand, four miles east of the Bill, which at low water is covered by over 14 feet of water. The Shambles Light lies a mile east of the shoal, in 15 fathoms of water, where the sixteenth vessel to be anchored at this spot was withdrawn and replaced by a LANBY [Large Automatic Navigation Buoy] in 1972.

This cost £3,000 a year to keep on station whereas the lightship was then costing £29,000 in annual bills. It had been built for Trinity House by Philip and Son of Dartmouth [1954] with a red hull, light-tower amidships, and its "SHAMBLES" name in big white capital letters along each side.

The first Shambles Lightship was anchored at this point on 1 September 1859. Trinity House provided these statistics of the final ship and its lighting signature: "It is 137 feet in length with a 25 feet beam and a tonnage of 345 tons. The light uses a system of mirrors in conjunction with a number of 100-volt 350-watt lamps. The light has a range of 25 miles and is shown at a height of 40 feet above sea level and the light character is two white flashes every 30 seconds."

The Shambles: its last Lightship.

Sheep – see entry for **Portland Sheep**, being the name of the island's rare breed.

Slapton Sands Massacre – the loss of 638 American soldiers and seamen, en route to Devon, occurred off Portland on the night of 27 April 1944, as I have recorded in *D-Day Dorset*.

A convoy of eight American tank landing ships [LSTs], taking part in the big Exercise Tiger practice landings at Slapton Sands, Devon, were intercepted by E-boats as they ventured across Lyme Bay, out into the English Channel:

"Motor torpedo boats of the 5th and 9th Schnellboot Flotillas ran amok amongst the Americans off the Portland end of the Chesil Beach, which is known locally, and in the works of Thomas Hardy, as Deadman's Bay from the memory of earlier shipwreck calamities.

"A total of 441 United States soldiers have been killed or drowned, together with 197 seamen; *LST507* and *LST531* are sunk with the loss of twelve tanks; *LST289* is damaged by a torpedo.

"The coastal gun batteries at Blacknor, Portland, prepared to open fire, but the American commander ordered them not to do so, in view of the number of his men who were in the water. The E-boats withdrew on the arrival of a corvette, HMS *Azalra*, and HMS *Saladin*, followed by HMS *Onslow*."

The dead would be stacked in piles on Castletown Pier in Portland Naval Dockyard. Offshore, teams of Navy divers worked for days to recover the identity discs from the other bodies, to account for all the missing and give Allied Naval Headquarters the welcome news that none had been fished out alive from the sea by the Germans and taken prisoner. Confirmation of their demise was accompanied by immense feelings of relief. 'This cloud's silver living,' as it was put in a secret memorandum, was the assurance that the invasion plans were still secret.

The Small Mouth – the estuary of the Fleet is the crossing point from the mainland to Portland (SY 667 762). The first Ferry Bridge was timber-built in 1839, and replaced by an iron bridge in 1896, which suffered terminal corrosion and sinkage and was replaced in the mid-1980s.

Before the bridging there was a chain-ferry operating here, at the end of the lane from Wyke Regis, powered by a horse plodding around a capstan. The wire was in a circuit, through the water attached to the boat, with the return length on pulley and in mid-air. The passage boat, it was called, and people in Wyke Regis still refer to Small Mouth and Ferry Bridge as "down Passage".

The former factory opposite the

Ferrybridge Hotel, then known as the Royal Victoria Hotel, was a major naval munitions plant in the two world wars – the Whitehead Torpedo Works. Small Mouth has Britain's only known colony of the Mediterranean scaly cricket, *Mogoplistes squamiger*. It was confirmed as a British species in 1955 after Bernard C. Pickard found five adults at the high-tide mark. They live under pebbles between the tide lines; a most unusual environment for a cricket.

Smith – school cleaner **Judith Smith** [born 1943] of Portland won £2 million in the fourth biggest pools win ever recorded [1993]. She quit her £38-a-week job to "give someone else the chance to earn a few bob".

Smuggling – more than 150 Portlanders passed through Dorchester Prison in the early 19th century as the great smuggling era was brought to a close by Customs and Excise officers and a gradual liberalisation in tarrifs and trade. Many were caught by the *Eagle* revenue cutter which notched up a particular run of successes in the 1820s. Most were sentenced to six months though usually only one month would actually be served.

Invariably they were quarrymen or fishermen, or both, and many of the island's traditional family names occur time and again in the *Calendar of Prisoners in Dorchester Gaol* – Attwooll, Bennett, Byatt, Champ, Charles, Comben, Flann, Miller, Pearce, Stone, Sweet, Way, and White.

Women played their full part, in both the offences and the time-serving, with concealment of the spirits and other smuggled goods being their main contribution.

Hiding holes were constructed by quarrymen beside the rocky beach at the foot of steep cliffs in Clay Ope, a spot as remote and inaccessible as any on the island (SY 681 722). Temporary stone hideouts were constructed in working quarries and an underground bunker was discovered in Will Stone's garden.

Southwell – Portland's southern hamlet grew up around the junction of the east and west roads for the final mile to Portland Bill. Beside its green lay the island's South Well (SY 687 701).

A Methodist Chapel was built on the east side of the junction in 1849. St Andrew's Avalanche Memorial Church was built immediately north of the ancient well in 1879. Between them, to the west of the junction, stands the Eight Kings' Inn which is said to have been given its name by a well-travelled Victorian landlord who knew of hostelries called the Seven Kings, but none with a larger number of monarchs. The modern village has extended westwards for half a mile to the remnants of Lawnsheds open fields beside the compound on the cliffs, enclosing the Admiralty Underwater Weapons Establishment.

Spy scandal – see entry for **Portland Spies**.

Sterrha degeneraria – the Portland Ribbon Wave, is one of Britain's rarest moths. It is only otherwise known from Torbay and central Europe.

Stone trade – the following paragraphs narrate some of the milestones of Portland's premier industry, chronicled in diary form.

1303: Considerable quantities of Portland stone are being used at Exeter Cathedral, for claves [the keys on bosses], cappings of the North Tower pinnacles and battlements, and for some string courses and ashlar. The Fabric Rolls note the payment of ten shillings "For carriage of a barge load of stones from Portland" and "For 18 large stone brought at Portland for bosses together with 60 bases and capitals and their transport by sea, £4 16s. 8d."

1347: Portland stone is being shipped to London for the building of the Royal Palace beside the Thames at Westminster.

1349: Portland stone is again being shipped to London for the

building of the new London Bridge, work on which will extend well into next year. [*This was to be the last major use of Portland stone until it returned to favour in the 17th century. Purbeck marble, also from Dorset, overshadowed Portland stone in the Middle Ages.*]

1600s: It has been noticed that "the present mode of drawing stone is most distressing to the horses" on the Island of Portland in Dorsetshire. In particular there are what they call Ape horses, "sometimes [*these*] two horses are made to drag behind when going downhill to the castle [*Castletown pier*] but it is now a more general and better practice to have stones dragged behind in chains and on slides to stop the carriages from going too fast down the precipices."

1622: The King's Pier is now completed on the north-east shore of the Island of Portland, for the shipment of stone to Whitehall. Work started in 1619 and has cost £700.

1620s: Large quantities of Portland stone are being shipped to London for the building of the Duke of Richmond's House at Holborn, and for York House which is being built for the Duke of Buckingham.

1635: Peter Mundy, a Cornishman, has visited the Island of Portland this July to oversee the working of a great deal of stone for the repair of [*the old, pre-Fire*] St Paul's Cathedral: "I went to the hewers of stone, which was carried for the reparation of St Paules Church in London. There were about 200 workemen, some hewing out of the cliffe alofte, some squaringe, some carryeing down, others ladeing. Some stones were ready squared and formed, of 9, 10 and 11 tonnes weight, as they said; some of they ready squared aloft and sent down in Carts made of purpose."

1635: Peter Mundy, the Cornish traveller, visited the isle of Portland in July and has made these observations about the great shells in its stone-beds [the first recorded note on the island's fossil beds]: "On the Cleaves, two or three fathom above full sea mark, are stores of great oyster shells; not as others growing or sticking fast to the rock, but incorporated into the same. The reason may be that those places in former times were under water, ouse, or mud, where those shellfishes did breed and feed."

1666, November: Sir John Denham [1615-69], the king's Surveyor General of Works, came to see the famous freestone quarries at Portland and approached to within a mile of them at the Small Mouth ferry passage. There he was seized with a distemper of madness and turned back for London where he told Charles II that he was the Holy Ghost. His deputy, Christopher Wren, is proceeding with the demolition of the ruins of London.

1675: Charles II has granted to the Dean and Chapter of St Paul's the right to raise stone on his Island of Portland in Dorsetshire for the building of their new Cathedral. The quarrying operations are under the control of their Surveyor and architect Christopher Wren.

1698: A meeting was held in London on Friday 20 January, attended by the Archbishop of Canterbury, the Bishop of London, the Dean of St Pauls, Christopher Wren, and others at which it was agreed that a contract should be prepared with Thomas Gilbert requiring him "to provide and ship off such Portland stones ... as he shall from time to time be directed by the Surveyor" for the purpose of rebuilding St Paul's Cathedral. It also ordered that "the said Gilbert shall make or cause to be made a substantial and good way leading from the quarries to the pier [*King's Pier, half a mile south-east from the present Castletown Pier*] in the said Island as he shall be directed, for the sume of £500, and to keep the same in good and sufficient repairs at the rate of £40 per annum." [*The original minute is preserved in the company archives of the Bath and Portland Group.*]

1700: The dome of the new St Paul's Cathedral is not yet started, but to Michaelmas the rebuilding of the church has taken 76,000 tons of stone. 50,322 tons of this has come from the Island of Portland in Dorsetshire, at a total cost of

£28,065 16s 7^3/$_4$d for the stone and £28,951 2s 8d for its freight. Much of this stone has been provided by Thomas Gilbert, an eminent member of the London Masons Company.

1701, 26 November: Sir Christopher Wren [1632-1723], who has passed through Weymouth many times whilst visiting the Portland quarries, has been elected member of Parliament for the town.

1710: Sir Christopher Wren watched from the ground as his son Christopher was hoisted in a bucket 360 feet into the sky, above the dome of St Paul's Cathedral, to lay its topmost piece of Portland stone.

1766: Quarrymen at Portland have not worked for some time and are endeavouring to get a shilling a ton more for their stone. They are finding their working tools carting a third more and the quarries increasingly expensive to work. If they cannot get more money they must leave off trade.

1804: Rev John Skinner of Camerton, near Bath, describes in his journal the methods of hauling stone on Portland: "... large hewn stones lie scattered in all directions; indeed the quarries worked on the island are prodigious and the mode of conveying the ponderous masses down the steep unavoidably arrests the attention of the stranger. The blocks being placed on a strong wooden carriage with solid wheels apportionate to the weight they are to sustain, two horses are harnessed on before and one and sometimes two behind, the latter being supplied with strong breaching, in order to act as drawbacks to the carriage, and prevent it running with too great velocity down the steep. Indeed the sagacity and exertions of these poor animals in this arduous employment is really astonishing; they squat down on their launches and suffer themselves to be dragged for many yards, struggling with all their strength against the weight that forces them forward. To one unaccustomed to the sight it appears as though their limbs must inevitably be dislocated or their sinews cracked by the violence of their exertions. Indeed one compassionates these poor creatures the rather, as all this labour might easily be obviated by the simple construction of a railroad" [*which was to take place in 1826*].

1887: the colossal Verne Citadel above the Harbour of Refuge at Portland has been completed and will carry this year on its datestone. Though work has been in progress for longer than many Portlanders can remember. Those who are long in the tooth will recall that it was in 1860 that 'Tophill' began to change its shape.

1890: Convicts on Portland are cutting the stone for the foundations of the new headquarters of the Metropolitan Police which will replace Scotland Yard. The building, on a site beside the Thames Embankment to the east of the Houses of Parliament, has been designed by Mr Norman Shaw RA.

Stonecrop – see entry for **Portland Stonecrop**.

Stopes – contraception pioneer **Dr Marie Stopes** [1880-1958] had become the country's youngest doctor of science in 1905, but it is not as a paleobotanist that she is remembered. In 1921 she founded Britain's first family planning clinic, the Mothers' Clinic for Constructive Birth Control, and chose Portland for a holiday home. This was the derelict Avice's Cottage at Wakeham – a Portland rarity as it is thatched – which had been mentioned by Thomas Hardy in his story of *The Well-Beloved*. She would later give the cottage to the island, for use as a museum (SY 697 713).

Meanwhile, through the 1920s, she brought out a stream of books on her chosen subject and became its leading pundit. *Married Love* of 1918 was followed by *Wise Parenthood and Radiant Motherhood* [1920]; *Contraception: its Theory, History and Practice* [1923]; *Sex and the Young; Enduring Passion* [1928] and *Sex and Religion* [1929].

Her own life failed to run the rails of textbook romance. Marie's first kiss did not come until the age of twenty-four. She married the Canadian botanist R. R. Gates in 1911 but obtained an annulment in 1916 on the claim of non-consummation. She then married the aviator Humphrey Verdon Roe [1878-1949] from the famous family of A. V. Roe and the Avro planemaking company. His money launched the family planning clinics and in 1923 he gave Marie her only son, Harry Verdon Stopes-Roe, on whom she would inflict a bizarre choice of clothing, non-education, and the cruel interference in his choice of a mate on the grounds that the girl was shortsighted and therefore genetically unfit for breeding.

By the time Harry was conceived the pair had moved to Portland's former Higher or Upper Lighthouse (SY 677 693). She refused to wear a bra or corset and threw her physical energy into swimming the treacherous tide-race off Portland Bill which one day almost claimed her life.

Portlanders would remember her wild red hair and recall with distaste the open philandering with young men. She exalted them in *Love Songs for Young Lovers* [1939], by which time the morality of the public Stopes, that of the string of books, was only a memory or less. H. V. Roe added a sad postscript to them with a letter written in the "Old Lighthouse" at Portland Bill:

"Five years ago when I told you I wanted no more sex union and that I should not object if you decided to have a lover to replace my deficiency – you were very hurt and answered that it was unthinkable. Now that you have suffered sex deprivation for all these years you may feel differently, and I wish to put it on record that if you did it would not in any way alter our existing relations ... as I have long considered a wife whose husband is incapable of coitus has every right to supplement his deficiency without breaking up the home."

Marie apparently dictated it. She was ahead of her time in managing two failed marriages and for setting the 20th century ethos that sex is a gift for enjoyment that seldom has to be complicated by procreative considerations. It was all a bit risqué for Portlanders, but this harsh landscape captured her heart and at the age of 78 her ashes would be cast by Harry from Portland Bill into the waters from which she had once been so lucky to escape.

Straits – between Easton and Wakeham with two clusters of 18th century houses (numbers 11 to 17), opposite the parish church of All Saints, with a datestone for "John Stevens 1734" and later rebuilt at the top into three-storeys (SY 693 718). Part of the house was the home of quarryman William Nelson [1711-70] and wife Jane, which seems to have been where Methodist pioneer Charles Wesley [1707-88] stayed on the night of 4 June 1746 and preached the following day.

The Strip – the matelot term for their special piece of Castletown, Portland; the first line of somewhat tacky buildings that are the beginnings of the civilian world.

The following potted description may soon fade into history following the closure of the Royal Navy dockyard. It is The Strip as it was rather than you may find it.

There's the office of the Naval Welfare organisation and the Base Chaplain, opposite St Paul's Church, and one of the earliest slot-machine laundries (SY 688 743). Whereon come the boozers, many with pennants and other nautical memorabilia, including the Albert Inn, the Breakwater Hotel, the Sailors Return (now an annexe to the Breakwater), the Portland Roads Hotel, and the Jolly Sailor. That little list tends to outgun the opposition, the "Sally Ann", as the Salvation Army Red Shield Hostel is known.

Sandwiched between the three-storey late Victorian and Edwardian facades are reminders that these are the Navy's watering holes –

building such as HM Customs House, shipping agents, and Grieves and Hawkes of Savile Row for the stylish officer.

Submarine tragedies – underwater warships were in vogue for the European navies before the First World War, and by its outbreak Britain alone had a hundred. Portland became established as a key base and it was inevitable that Dorset would suffer a major disaster. It is not unfair to say that the public's imagination was gripped by the horrific concept of men trapped in a "sewer pipe" on the sea-bed and facing an utterly hopeless end.

When Dorset's first submarine accident occurred it was of another kind. The huge battlecruiser HMS *Resolution* collided with British submarine *L-24* to the west of Portland in Lyme Bay [10 January 1924]. It was like a baby being run over by a lorry. The submarine was sent to the bottom and there were no survivors among the forty-three officers and men.

By the beginning of the 1930s submarine disasters were becoming almost commonplace and only a month after the loss of the *Poseidon* the Admiralty had to issue another ominous statement:

"News has been received this evening that Submarine *M-2* dived about 10.30 this morning off Portland and since then no further

communication has been received from her."

The day was 26 January 1932 and that night the Admiralty released a second statement: "An object, believed to be Submarine *M-2* , has been located three miles west off Portland Bill, in seventeen fathoms on a sandy bottom. Salvage craft and divers have been sent from Portsmouth.

M-2 had been completed by Vickers in October 1918 and armed with a monster 12-inch calibre gun taken from an obsolete *Majestic* class battleship. In 1927 the gun was removed and *M-2* was recommissioned as an aircraft carrier.

She carried a catapult-launched reconnaissance seaplane. Unusual as this seems now, it was less surprising at the time, as before the First World War the Bristol-Burney X-craft was designed in a collapsible form for submarines, and in 1916 two Sopwith Schneider planes were housed in submarine *E-22*. The plane hanger caused the loss of *M-2*.

A steamer captain approaching Portland on the morning of 26 January 1932 saw a submarine apparently dive stern first. On 29 January the navy had to admit that "it is no longer possible to hope for the rescue of the officers and men on board". The precise position of the submarine was fixed on 3 February and divers raised its biplane five days later.

Efforts began to raise the submarine. Dogged by bad weather on the surface, salvage divers also encountered numerous problems as they worked. Hatches were found to be open and more required sealing than had at first been estimated. Strong tides swept the men away from the wreck.

After all this, the lifting attempts almost succeeded, and the *M-2* was brought to within eighteen feet of the surface. Salvage had to be finally abandoned on 8 September 1932 and today *M-2* lies on the seabed with her crew entombed.

There were the usual arguments about what had happened. H. F. King concludes an article in Aeroplane Monthly in May 1973 with the modern verdict of what caused the end to a chapter of naval ingenuity: "Scant doubt remains concerning *M-2*'s fate ... the inner hatch to the hanger was probably open together with the hanger doors themselves, thereby admitting water to the hull. Probably through a misinterpreted order, the sea had indeed, gone 'right down into the boat'.

M-2's sister ship, *M-1*, had already had her accident, further to the west. Her crew are entombed off Start Point. She had been completed in time for war service off the Dardanelles and was carrying her battleship gun when she met her end in collision with a steamship on 12 November 1925.

Portland Harbour itself became the scene of a submarine disaster in 1955. There was an explosion in the torpedo bay of HMS *Sidon* and she sank twenty minutes later, drowning thirteen men still on board. *Sidon* was raised after the accident and sank again, deliberately this time, in 1957, to become an asdic target off Portland.

The Tabernacle – temporary stone-built Anglican church in Wakeham, used after the abandoning of St Andrew's [1753], during the lengthy building of St George's in Reforne [1754-66]. It was "built beside Edward Cooper's house, which was apparently the last building at the bottom of Wakeham Street, on the east side".

In order to keep it in a consecrated place, the communion table remained in the now ruinous St Andrew's being brought back and forth as required. This led to an annual payment of a shilling, recorded in the church accounts: "For carrying ye table to and from ye Tabernacle concerning ye communion."

Thames – Penzance steamer, heading from Newlyn to London, which rammed into Tar Rocks (SY 681 725) in dense fog [2 January 1891]. Her crew of twelve escaped ashore. The vessel carried granite roadstone and tin ingots which can still be found among the offshore rocks.

HMS *Tiger* – veteran of the Battle of Jutland [31 May 1916], became the Royal Navy's principal gunnery practice ship, based at Portland and firing offshore in the Lyme Bay and English Channel ranges [1924-29].

Tombolo – see entry for **Chesil Beach**.

Torpedo Depot – established in the new Royal Naval Dockyard at Portland [1901] but transferred to Bincleaves Breakwater, Weymouth, during the Great War [1915]. Whitehead Torpedo Works, on the Weymouth side of Small Mouth passage (SY 668 763) was established by Robert Whitehead [1891] and supplied this weapon, which Whitehead originally developed at Fiume in Italy [1867].

Tout Quarries – little except the splendid Lano's Bridge is now left of the perfect collection of large-scale workings and mineral railways on the north-west top of Portland (SY 685 729). The ravines between the 18th and 19th century workfaces were colonised by orchids and other botanical rarities. Though the north part of the area was used as a setting for a Sculpture Park open-air art display [1985] it had already suffered widespread disturbance and destruction to provide buildings for coast defence work at West Bay, Bridport [1983]. The southern part of the quarries, together with its cliff-edge features that combined industrial archaeology with a breathtaking view, has been bulldozed into mediocrity.

The workings formerly extended from the top of West Weares, south of Priory Corner and from the cliff-edge inland as far as the Wide Road. These were bounded on the southern side by the Trade Quarries which extended from Furze Close Lawn, midway between St George's Church and Priory Corner, for the remainder of the western cliffs as far south as Goslins and Dungeness, north-west of Reforne.

"Tout" is an ancient word for "a lookout". William Lisle Bowles noted in his *Dissertation on the Celtic Deity Teutes* [1828] that "most of the hills of the sea-coast, and through Dorsetshire, are still pronounced Teuts [Toots] by the common people".

Trinity House navigation beacon – pyramid-shaped landmark at Portland Bill. Erected in 1844 to replace a 30 foot high column. The "T.H." on its side stands for Trinity House, not Thomas Hardy, which might seem like stating the obvious but I have had several letters on the point over the years from Dorset County Magazine readers.

The stone is a navigation beacon. While the lighthouse is used to warn distant shipping a beacon is a danger signal for inshore boats and is used for obtaining a precise fix on the charts. Beacon, in this sense, is a term for any structure, even a landmark like a church steeple, that can be used by navigators to check their position.

G. S. Thomson, the information officer at Trinity House, confirmed to me in 1973 that it was their stone. He looked it up in a full report of all British lights and beacons, carried out in 1861, which gave the Portland Bill stone as "date of erection unknown". It was news to him that it carried a date.

I pointed out that their Victorian surveyors could be excused for not noting the 1844, given that unlike me they could not get such information from a telephone call.

Trumani (being oceanic earthquake-caused "tidal waves") – see entry for **Flood disasters**.

U-boat – the first U-boat kill off the Dorset coast in the Second World War came only 40 hours after the declaration of hostilities. The new K-class destroyer HMS *Kelly*, leading the 5th Destroyer Flotilla from Portland, depth-charged an enemy submarine in Lyme Bay [5 September 1939]. Substantial wreckage came to the surface. *Kelly* had earlier missed the tracks of two torpedos fired at her, in Weymouth Bay, by only 30 or 40 yards.

U-14 – nearly claimed by the Royal Navy off Portland Bill in a collision that nearly coincided with one of the fiftieth anniversaries of the Second World War [25 January 1995].

The 500-ton diesel-electric German submarine was at periscope depth when it was hit by the starboard propeller of the 4,400-ton frigate HMS *Battleaxe*. Two torpedo tubes and a ballast tank were damaged but the pressurised hull was not ruptured. Both vessels returned to Portland naval base, from where they had been taking part in war games.

U-249 – the first German U-boat to surrender at the end of the Second World War. She had signalled her intention to the Royal Navy and a rendezvous was arranged in Weymouth Bay, prior to her being led into Portland Harbour by the frigates HMS *Amethyst* and *Magpie* [10 May 1945].

U-269 – sunk between Start Point and Portland by HMS *Bickerton*, as she attempted to stalk a Normandy supply convoy [25 June 1944].

U-776 – attempted to surrender at Freshwater, Isle of Wight, at the end of the war in Europe but the offer was refused [16 May 1945] and she was redirected to Portland Harbour.

U-825 – followed *U-249* into Portland Harbour as Grand-Admiral Karl Doenitz's submarine fleet surrendered at the close of World War Two [10 May 1945].

U-1023 – came into Weymouth Harbour as the German underwater fleet gave itself up to the Royal Navy at the end of the Second World War [10 May 1945]. She was the third German submarine to surrender and joined *U-249* and *U-825* in Portland Harbour.

U-1191 – German submarine, destroyed by the frigates HMS *Affleck* and *Balfour*, as she attempted to shadow the Normandy supply routes, between Portland and Start Point [24-25 June 1944].

Unexploded bomb: defused by Captain Michael Lobb.

UB-74 – German submarine of the First World War, UB standing for Underwater-Boat, sunk by the armed yacht *Lorna* west of Portland Bill, in Lyme Bay [26 May 1918]. Three depth charges were released as the submarine attempted to dive after being caught sailing on the surface.

Underwater Weapons Establishment – see entry for **Admiralty Underwater Weapons Establishment**.

Unexploded bomb – Portland's famous relic of the Second World War, a 1,000-lb device thought to have been dropped by a Heinkel bomber in 1942, was discovered under a football pitch [March 1995]. Some 4,000 people were evacuated from their homes for a 31-hour operation by a Royal Engineers Bomb Disposal team, lead by Captain Michael Lobb [born 1968].

He brought it to a successful conclusion with a controlled explosion that was heard more than two miles away on Portland Bill [08.15 hours, 3 April 1995].

Upper Lighthouse – see entry for **Higher Lighthouse**.

Verne Camp – see entry for **Hill-fort**.

Verne Citadel now **Portland Prison** – the great Victorian fortress on the top of The Verne above Castletown and Fortuneswell, Portland (SY 692 737). It was convict-built [1860-87] on a strategic site that had the double banks of an Iron Age hill-fort and was already staked out for fortification when the Royal Commission on the Defence of the United Kingdom reported to Prime Minister Viscount Palmerston [1860] at the time of the Franco-Prussian War.

Designed by Captain Crossman of the Royal Engineers, it is colossal in scale and great in area, some fifty acres, with the steep cliffs topped with low-profile wide walls that are just about as impregnable as anywhere in northern Europe, and barracks for 1,000 troops. Their accommodation was considered shell and bomb-proof, being beneath vaulted brickwork and a semi-circle of stone arches – covered above with rock and grassed into a steep slope that drops to a level central drill-ground. Everything was within the walls, from a hospital to gymnasium and cricket and tennis lawns.

Huge 32-ton rifled muzzle-loaded cannon were emplaced in the barbettes overlooking the approaches to Portland Harbour. There were nine fixed and ten mobile artillery pieces in 1888. On the other side, however, the

Verne Citadel: the great dry moat.

Verne Citadel: 1881 datestone on what is now Portland Prison, with Stephen Taylor just visiting.

vulnerable element in the scheme was the flat top of the island. Here there were more gun batteries, beyond the Citadel, but between them is a ditch of immense proportions.

This Victorian dry-moat has sheer sides, 120 feet wide, and is 70 feet deep at the eastern end. Kestrels nest on the sides. A winding staircase snakes underground through the solid stone interior of the Citadel to emerge at a door in the bottom of the ditch. Here there was a rifle-range.

The ditch was the largest single source of stone – no less than 1,500,000 tons – for the harbour's Outer Breakwater. Anyone chancing to slip from its edge fell to his death, as was the case with a soldier of the Dorsetshire Regiment [22 November 1887].

"Makes you hold your stomach," a Portlander remarked to me. "A man named Verne built it all and when they finished the ditch he threw himself in!"

Unfortunately for the story, it was Verne in 1608 and Ferne in 1321. The Dorset dialect turns 'f' into 'v'. Though I do take issue with placename expert A. D. Mills in saying that the word can mean "wooded". There is about as much of a chance for tree-planting on Verne's mountain-top as there would be of having a forestry programme in the Falklands.

"1881" is its datestone. Verne was an infantry barracks from 1903 and its guns were removed in 1906. It became an infantry training centre in 1937 and the last military unit, appropriately Royal Engineers, left when the Home Office Prison Service took over in 1948. It currently holds 520 men and has medium security status.

von Dalwigk – "Stuka" leader **Hauptmann Friedrich-Karl Freiherr von Dalwigk zu Lichtenfels**, the 33-year-old Staffelkapitan of I Gruppe, Stukageschwader 77, was shot down in his Junkers Ju87 and killed over the sea off Portland [9 July 1940]. The kill was claimed by Pilot Officer David Moore Crook, flying a Spitfire from RAF Warmwell. Von Dalwigk, who had joined the Luftwaffe in 1933, would be posthumously awarded the Knight's Cross [21 July 1940].

Wakeham – the distinctive wide street in the middle of the island, southwards from the Straits to the gateway into the grounds of Pennsylvania Castle (SY 695 716). Most of its older buildings survive, dating from the 17th and 18th century, with characteristic porches and stone-mullioned windows. Many have fine blocks of squared ashlar. The gem at the southern end, Avice's Cottage, is dated 1640 and almost unique on the island in retaining a thatched roof. It now houses part of Portland Museum.

Waitara – iron-built sailing ship of the New Zealand Shipping Company, which sank off Portland Bill after being in collision with her sister-ship, *Hurunui* [6 September 1882]. They were sailing together, out of London, and heading down-Channel. There were two impacts, two minutes apart, and 26 crew and passengers were drowned as the *Waitara* went down.

War Anchorage and Trawler Station – the Admiralty designation of Portland Harbour during the Great War [1914-18], controlling sea-area XIII. The battleships and cruisers of the Home Fleet were gathered at Portland [8-29 July 1914] preceding the declaration of hostilities, with Admiral Sir George Callaghan, the Commander-in-Chief, being summoned by train to Whitehall where he was told that he was being replaced by Admiral Sir John Jellicoe.

The fleet was meanwhile putting to sea, ordered to turn left in the English Channel and make for Scapa Flow, in the Orkney Islands, and war-stations.

The battleship HMS *Agamemnon* remained at Portland and would join the 5th Battle Squadron of the Second Fleet after war was declared [4 August 1914]. Armed trawlers of the Auxiliary patrol were also mobilised, to protect merchant shipping, and anti U-boat

precautions were taken. The obsolete ironclad battleship HMS *Hood* was scuttled to block the South Ship Channel (SY 702 745) of Portland Harbour [November 1916]. Boom defence nets were opened and closed to prevent submarines slipping past the Chequered Fort, as its East Ship Channel became the main entrance to the harbour. Similar booms, usually kept closed, secured the North Ship Channel.

Twenty-eight armed trawlers were based at Portland by the time of the Armistice [11 November 1918], with myriad other patrol and support vessels, including several requisitioned paddle-steamers which – because of their shallow draught – were excellent for inshore mine and wreck clearance.

The end of the war saw the gathering of more than 200 of these vessels [December 1918] for demobilisation and return to their civilian owners.

HMS **Warrior** – Edwardian Portland was host to every type of craft in the evolution of British warships, "from the old wooden walls with their spreading white sails, to the latest *Dreadnought* creation, a sort of monstrous floating fort," and even the occasional primitive submarine.

The earlier transitional battleships used steam auxiliary power only. When under sail, one funnel was lowered out of sight, and the screw propeller lifted from the water. Steam at that time was regarded as little more than emergency propulsion for time of calm.

In the 1920s it was reported that one of Portland's veteran warships, the unique HMS *Warrior* – "for many years the guardship in the harbour, and considered the most pleasing model of the armour-plated, sailrigged class" – was to be preserved in Portsmouth Harbour. That indeed came to pass, but not until 1986; meantime she was used as a berthing jetty at Milford Haven.

HMS *Warrior* was built in 1859-60 as the world's first iron-clad warship and was powered both by steam and 48,400 square feet of canvas. These sails required a crew of 600 men. The upper deck is four hundred feet long. Below there were 80 guns. Her introduction met with some resistance and moved the goalposts of naval warfare.

Wasp – principal anti-submarine helicopter of the Royal Navy for a quarter of a century, during which it was the commonplace aircraft in Portland's sky [1963-88]. Their farewell flypast, in formation across Portland Harbour, was carried out by ten Wasps of 829 Naval Air Squadron on 11 January 1988.

Water supply – Portland placenames commemorate the former importance of its wells, and even Easton Pond was not condemned as a source of drinking water until 1871. Work started on an island borehole, at Southwell, in 1890 but it had to be abandoned on completion [May 1895] after £6,000 had been spent on breaking through the strata into Kimmeridge clay which turned the water brackish.

Then, with Portland now being of national strategic importance, the search turned inland. A supply was found up the valley from Upwey Wishing Well and pumped to a 500,000-gallon hilltop reservoir at 545 feet above sea level [1898].

From here, via a ten mile main of 10-inch pipe, a high pressure supply extended across the whole island, including Tophill and the highest point on Verne Hill, at 495 feet above sea level. A larger booster reservoir was constructed at Verne Yeates [1902] but is only partly filled, due to a crack. A secondary pumping station was later established at Friar Waddon, north-west of Weymouth, below Ridgeway Hill.

Weare – Her Majesty's Prison *Weare*, a 480-berth vessel, was shipped across the Atlantic and moored in Portland Harbour [13 March 1997]. Previously named *The Resolution* she had been a drug rehabilitation centre on the Hudson River, New York; *Weare* is the Portland name for a rocky cliff.

Its category C inmates lifted the island's prison population to 1,500. The vessel's arrival triggered Dickensian allusions to the Victorian hulks. Though she was the first and only accommodation for convicted prisoners in the 20th century, republican detainees and internees had been held in HMS *Maidstone*, moored in Belfast Harbour in the 1970s, and Sealink ferry *Earl William* housed immigration detainees at Harwich [1987].

HMP *Weare* is the length of a football pitch, piled to the height of four double-decker buses with rows of metal boxes, five floors high for most of its superstructure. Facilities include squash courts, swimming pools, a library, chapel, and a mosque.

Costing £3.5 million, the vessel was brought across the Atlantic on the colossal cargo barge *Giant 4*.

The Weares – name for sections of Portland's rocky undercliff, invariably covered with stone-waste. Always used for land on the slopes rather than for the flat clifftop above.

Often the Ordnance Survey map gives them collective names such as West Weares and East Weares but on the ground each was subdivided, mentally if not physically, into a series of lesser Weares. For instance, West Weares began at Chesil Cove with Killick's Hill Weare, and moves on to Flower's Weare and Pranker's Weare. Next are Pitt's Weare and the more extensive Silverwell Weare. Knight's Weare completes the collection.

Similarly, around Penn's Weare on the coast north of Church Ope on the opposite shore, maps fail to name other Weares of similar size that lie on each side. These start at Church Point with Church Point Weare and Andrew's Weare above. Then comes Penn's Weare, North Wall Weare, and Outer Weare, with Gilbert's Weare extending along the foot of the steep "Touts" above them. Sue Flew's Weare and Durdle Weare bring you to the site of Durdle Pier, with Hellier's Weare on the north side of it.

The Well-Beloved – Thomas Hardy's novel is set on Portland, in three episodes that cover the period 1857-97, with the ending being in what was the future at the time of publication [magazine serial, 1892; book form 1897]. Jocelyn Pierston, a Portland sculptor who finds his fortune in London, returns to his native isle to fulfil his ideal of womanhood. Each of his infatuations, with successive generations of the Caro family, fails to reach the altar.

Hardy's name for Portland is the "Isle of Slingers" from the ancient use of its beach-pebbles as slingstones.

Wesley – evangelist **John Wesley** [1703-91] visited Portland [1746], where a Methodist community had been founded by William Nelson [1743]. Whilst lodging on the island, at Easton, he wrote "before preaching at Portland" a hymn that was inspired by the stone trade:

Come, O thou all-victorious Lord!
Thy power to make known;
Strike with the hammer of Thy word,
And break these hearts of stone.

Wesley probably preached in the old parish church of St Andrew, and certainly at a private house in the Straits, Easton.

Weston – Portland's Victorian new town grew up around the junction beside Weston Pond (SY 686 710). Weston is the street heading northwards, towards Reforne, and Weston Street goes east, to the grounds of Pennsylvania Castle.

Just north of Weston Corner and Coopers Place, Weston widens into Weston Green, with Providence Place and Gipsy Lane to the north-west. An 18th century house survives sub-divided.

Non-conformists provided a Wesleyan Chapel [1858] and a Primitive Methodist Chapel [1860]. A Wesleyan School was built in 1878, accommodating 227 pupils, and replaced by a new school in 1902.

Wigley – Navy flyer **Captain Anthony Wigley** was killed when his Wessex Mark V helicopter crashed on one of the breakwaters of Portland Harbour [3 December 1984].

Willowbank – a sailing ship, which sank near Portland [22 December 1895].

Windmills – water power was freely available in Dorset and windmills were consequently always uncommon. There are no beautiful wooden windmills to compare to the once plentiful examples in eastern England.

Significantly, the only two historic Dorset specimens which survive are on the dry and windswept top of Portland on the edge of a quarry at Easton (SY 691 714). Probably they were built in the 17th century. Strips of open fields run southward from the mills and across a shallow valley. The open field in which they stand is called Haylands and was formerly known as Droopfield. Both windmills are marked on a map of 1710 reproduced in John Hutchins's fulsome county history of Dorset.

Windmills are known in Britain from the 12th century, but the oldest surviving mills date from the 1600s. If you want clues to the former existence of Dorset windmills then you have only to look at placenames such as Windmill Knap and Windmill Barn

Windmill rarities: Portland has plenty of wind.

at Langton Matravers in Purbeck.

The Portland mills are built of stone and were first recorded on a map of 1626. They have traditionally been in the hands of the Pearce family. The sails last turned corn to grist (pronounced in Portland with a long 'i') at the turn of the century and some old people remember there was a stone-race beside one of the mills. A carriage ran to trim the sails by increasing wind resistance. The foundation of the mills are deep – with mortared pebbles that kept out rats.

I made the following notes on the mills in 1967:

South Mill: Height about 21 feet. Door opening 2ft. 3in. wide by 4ft high. Internal diameter of the circular tower is 13ft. at ground level. There are four openings in the wall about 5ft. above the floor and these are about 1ft. 6in. wide by a foot high. The wall, at the door, is 2ft. 5in. thick. The lower part of the mill was converted to a pill-box during the war.

Angel Mill: Height about 18 feet. There are two door openings; the north-west is 2ft. 4in. wide and 5ft. 1in. high and the south-east is 2ft. 6in. wide by 4ft. high. This mill, unlike the first, is open at the top and has internal widths of 12 feet (east to west) and 11 feet (north to south). The thickness of the wall at one door ranges from 2ft. 2in. to 2ft. 6in. Remains of the sail timbers rest on the top of the mill and the shaft which once worked the mill comes to within four feet of the ground. This central spindle is over two feet thick. Both these buildings are tower-mills and their condition is deteriorating.

Angel Mill is the northern windmill, on Green Hill, with South Mill on the other side of the unenclosed Cotton Fields.

Witchcraft – Portlanders were reluctant to renounce their traditional belief in witchcraft and indeed split from the Wesleyan church over the issue [1816]. The minister Rev Francis Derry, found himself with only half a congregation after an acrimonious confrontation with those who were said to have "The Power". Fifty were said to have admitted such beliefs: "Almost every event was supposed to be regulated by this evil power,

and every misfortune was attributed to the witch."

The result was the alternative chapel, built at Chiswell by witch-believing Methodists, and which became known as the Conjurer's Lodge. It was founded by Charles Whittle and Robert Hinde who took half of Derry's flock with them.

Woolf – for **Virginia Woolf**, then **Miss Virginia Steven**, see entry for the ***Dreadnought* Hoax**.

Wordsworth – **Captain John Wordsworth** [1772-1805], outward bound commanding the East Indiaman *Abergavenny*, was among more than 250 who drowned on the Shambles sandbanks, off the Bill, Portland, on 5 February 1805. The disaster had been caused by a pilot's error.

Elder brother William Wordsworth [1770-1850] was deeply distressed by his death and made many references to it in his poems. The *Happy Warrior*, inspired by the death of Lord Nelson later in the year, incorporates aspects of John's character. He is buried at Wyke Regis, Weymouth.

Wren – architect **Sir Christopher Wren** [1632-1723] picked up the pieces after the Great Fire of London in 1666, being appointed "Surveyor-general and principal architect for rebuilding the whole city; the cathedral church of St

Paul; all the parochial churches ... with other public structures." He would rebuild not in imitation of the mediaeval but on a grand and classical scale that would bring him his knighthood [1672] and establish Portland limestone as the nation's capital building stone, ahead of granite. Wren was elected as member of Parliament for Weymouth on 26 November 1701. In London in 1710 he watched from the ground as son Christopher was hoisted in a bucket 360 feet into the sky, above the dome, to lay the topmost piece of Portland stone to complete the exterior profile of St Paul's.

Wren's Wine Glass – the marking used by Christopher Wren for Portland stones personally selected for St Paul's Cathedral. Some surplus to requirement, or otherwise rejected, still lie on the island.

Wyatt – eminent architect **James Wyatt** [1746-1813] designed the graceful Bryanston House but only the stable-block survives from its conversion into a red-brick pile. Smaller, but intact, is the mock-Gothic and sham-fortification Pennsylvania Castle, Portland.

Young Offenders' Institution – previously known as The Borstal, after the location of the first such institution in Kent, started life as Portland Prison in 1848. Its austere five-storey lines dominate the end of the Grove (SY 702 726) and overlook the island's eastern shore at Folly Pier.

It was the top security gaol for category-one felons of the day who were headed by members of the Fenian Brotherhood, the predecessor to the Irish Republican Army. Those of its captured members who escaped the gallows were sent to Portland for long sentences of hard labour in the stone quarries. They produced *knobblers* – building blocks dressed on five sides and with only one face remaining rough.

Jeremiah O'Donovan Rossa was the most notorious of the Irish convicts held on the island in 1866-69. His release was brought forward after he had a letter smuggled to the press which told of horrific conditions, and by election in his absence as the member for Tipperary in the United Kingdom Parliament. Not that his future lay there. Having secured his freedom he led the Irish American pressure for Home Rule and survived an assassination attempt in which he was gunned down by a young British widow on the streets of New York.

As for the most notable Englishman held in these cells, Convict V.460, Jabez Balfour (ex-Member of Parliament for Burnley) arrived on 19 June 1896 at the pinnacle of white-collar crime for the victorian period. His fourteen years' penal servitude, of which eighteen months were spent on Portland, was imposed for company fraud and corruption. He had built a business empire upon a web of deceit that fell apart in 1892.

He fled to the Argentine but was extradited to the United Kingdom to stand trial at the Old Bailey.

Balfour's crime was ahead of its time, as was the way he would later articulate the problems of being a fallen pillar of Victorian society: "If the brutal warder of popular melodrama was ever a real person, he was to be found at Portland during my time there. That is many years ago now. Things have doubtless changed since then, but Portland as I knew it was a heart-breaking, soul-enslaving, brain-destroying hell upon earth. The tone of the officers' voices, their curt, dictatorial and offensive manner, their sneering laughs and gibes struck me as being in consonance with the place itself ... During our miserable hour of exercise the assistant warder who had charge of us on one occasion threw a stick down in our path and defied any man to pass it except on the left-hand side. I myself was twice reproved for looking up at the sky ... Once a prisoner in passing me smiled, the warder saw and was swift to shout, 'Now then Balfour, smiling is not allowed here'."

May some of these entries have brought you smiles – for even Dorset's island of stone can present a happy face.

Portland & Chesil Beach.

A PORTLAND TERRET